Mountain Villages

by
Alice Bullock

Sunstone Press
Santa Fe, New Mexico

SECOND EDITION
Revised and Enlarged

Printed in the United States of America

LIBRARY OF CONGRESS CATALOGING IN PUBLICATION DATA

Bullock, Alice, 1904–
    Mountain villages.

    Includes index.
    1. New Mexico—Description and travel—1951–
2. New Mexico—History, Local. 3. Villages—New Mexico.
I. Title.
F801.2.B84   1981   978.9'009'734   81-5687
ISBN: 0-913270-13-X   AACR2

Published in 1981 by
SUNSTONE PRESS
Post Office Box 2321
Santa Fe, New Mexico 87501

Contents

Acknowledgements

How does a writer acknowledge the help of a multitude of people? I stop to chat with a man plowing a field who does not tell me his name, only that his father tilled this field before him. I ask directions at a backdoor; the lady of the house fills not only that need but a cup of coffee and friendly information about the village. My Spanish is not good, nor is her English, but we became friends, for we share a love of the village.

Marsha Zucal has been an invaluable help and companion. Ruth McPherson has packed lunches, filled thermos bottles of coffee and lifted a flagging spirit. Both Marsha and Ruth share my love for the mountain homes and people. Belina and Leroy Ramirez, who took me to Viola and Tito Martinez – both couples tops in any capacity. Regina Cooke in Taos, Virginia Jennings at the State Library, so knowledgeable and understanding – as is the rest of the staff there.

The staff at *The New Mexican* – Jack Cox, Dick McCord, Chet Dinnell, John Bott, Bob Dimery, and heading the list, Ann Clark, who shared her strength and wisdom.

Most of all, of course, my gratitude to my husband, Dale, who helped with suggestions, ideas, never fussing about a neglected house, sketchy meals or no meal at all when Ma was late getting home. I am a very lucky gal, and I am the one who knows it. I sincerely hope readers enjoy this book for then all who helped will be, in small measure, repaid.

Some of these chapters were printed in *The New Mexican*.

Moun**tain Villages**

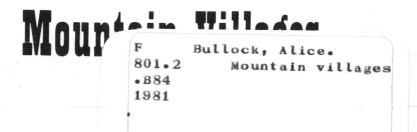

to all the
and o

Marsha Zu
who lo

Preface

Rural people all over the world are packing up their household goods and moving to urban centers. They don't really want to, nor do they relish "city" life. Changing times are inexorably forcing them to move. No longer can a man farm a small plot of land and provide for a family. Young people have to have jobs, and there are practically none in our mountain villages. They go away to college and do not return to farm Dad's ranchito. If they don't go to college, they find jobs as clerks, secretaries, filling station attendants – doing all the things that must be done, even while their hearts cry out for the clean air, the close relationships and the crimeless little towns that gave them a sense of belonging during their formative years. Sadly, they know that love doesn't conquer poverty, disease or ignorance.

Our mountain villages, so long a source of strength, are being kept partially alive by the older generation, but alone they cannot make the village thrive. Too soon the *camposanto* claims them, and, as they change their residence to the churchyards, another house goes blind with broken windows. Roofs, untended, leak streams of water and melted snow onto adobe walls. They slowly crumble and rejoin the soil from which they sprang. Each of them, in dying, diminishes all of us. Only a century ago rural population made up three-fourths of our country. Today 70 percent of all Americans live on 1.5 percent of the land.

Everything seems to work against the rural communities. Mechanization which villagers can't afford, brings the price for their products down to a level where they can't make ends meet. Orange colored school buses pluck their young from the side of the road where once their own schools gave cohesion to the community. Cities groan under the burden of too-fast growth and demands for more services. The "big" wages to be earned are not so big when the costs of shelter and food seem always to be more then they can make. Welfare rolls increase, and taxes proliferate.

We can't go back, and the rural exodus is not yet complete. Too little and too late we spit in the ocean. We can only, hopefully, remember.

Choice of villages for this book was completely haphazard. There are many, many more – each with its own personality, its own story. While nostalgia grips those who once lived in them, traffic jams, noise, pollution and taxes drive us up the walls. Government projects work on urban renewal, but few voices are raised for the cradle of our birth, the spawning ground of our nation – the village.

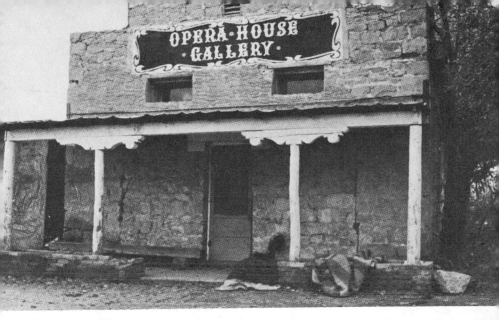

OLD OPERA HOUSE provides space for exhibiting artists.

I.

Little Rolling Hills

The "little rolling hills" of Cerrillos are dotted with low-growing pinon and pock marked with hundreds of holes, some shallow, some very deep — holes that are drift mines, cutting into the rock, gravel and soil in tunnels of mining and others going straight down with rotted timbering where men labored mightily to find a mother lode.

Cerrillos was once a boom town, with enough inhabitants to seriously challenge Santa Fe as the Territorial Capital. No one has yet found the mother lode that pulled not only miners and prospectors, but bookkeepers, butchers and businessmen from far places, all with one big dream — wealth. These men and their families came from everywhere, for GOLD!!! is a fever for which even today there is no antibiotic to alleviate the high temperature that it engenders. Men die, but not the dream.

Indians, who roamed these hills before the coming of the white man, dreamed too, but their dream was of the blue sky-stone — turquoise. Open mines, particularly on the slopes of Mount Chalchihuitl, have rewarded antiquarians with stone hammers that silently tell of perhaps a thousand years of mining for turquoise by the Indians. Ruins of old pueblos yield bits of Cerrillos turquoise that were trade items, for the turquoise from

1

the rolling hills was beautiful and brought (say the legends) good luck, for turquoise was a gift of the gods and a gift to them in ceremonials as well as a scrap under the pueblo wall to keep it from sagging and cracking. Another legend tells us that this blue stone is the heart of the mother of the twin war gods shattered when one of her sons killed the other while playing games of war. No ruins of prehistoric pueblos are located where the village of Cerrillos now stands, but the area is surrounded with them. Many of the Indians from this part of the country were among those who made the Palace of the Governors a pueblo when they successfully forced all the Spaniards, who were not slain, out of New Mexico during the Rebellion of 1680.

One story is told that the Spaniards who settled in the valley worked the Indians as slaves in the turquoise mines and that a mine cave-in killed a number of these slaves, sparking the rebellion. Indians are said to have filled in and concealed the mines to prevent the same thing from ever happening again. This would have been an enormous undertaking, for it has been estimated that at least 100,000 tons of waste rock had been dumped by the Indians before the Spaniards arrived.

After De Vargas reconquered New Mexico, Spaniards once again slowly settled the valley. The big boom in Cerrillos did not come until after 1880 with mining as the fuse. Gold was what they really wanted, but lead, zinc and coal were not to be despised. Panning gold takes water, and water was a scarce commodity. Trying to find a way to extract those shiney yellow flakes from the dirt brought the great inventor Thomas Edison to Cerrillos, though he was working on the soil at Golden. He was trying to do it with electromagnetism, for such a method worked wonderfully in his laboratory. But it wouldn't work out here! Eventually he found out that the gold-impregnated soil had to be completely dry, and building ovens to dry it out was not feasible. The coal veins at Madrid had not yet been discovered, and there simply wasn't enough piñon wood to do the job.

Edison lived at the old Palace Hotel while he worked in the area. Mining had caused four hotels, a bakery, jewelry store, 27 saloons, dance halls, a theater, pool halls, cantinas, grocery and general merchandise stores, the whole bit, to mushroom all over the flats. The coming of the railroad augmented the growth of the town, of course.

Myrtle Andrews Gere recalled that Edison had a flatbed wagon pulled up in Golden, and on it put his new invention, the gramophone, and played it for the crowd. It was an exciting event, a talking music box, complete with a morning glory horn and heavy cylinder records.

2

Fire was always a major threat in Cerrillos, and in 1890 a bad one sent 13 business buildings up in smoke. The Palace Hotel was destroyed by fire only a few years ago. After the Palace burned, the village finally got around to organizing a fire department.

Mary Tappero Mora watched through tear-dimmed eyes as the Palace Hotel burned. She was born in the hotel, and that fire was destroying a tangible symbol of her memories and those given her by her father and grandfather. There were 32 rooms in the old place, and every one a lodestone of old events. Not only Edison had stayed there, but Lew Wallace (author of *Ben Hur*) and Bradford Prince, among the good guys. A wounded Black Jack Ketchum, one of the bad guys, came in to the doctor's office, then in the hotel, and bled all over the floor. The stain was still there when the Palace burned. A despondent man who worked for Cash Entry mine hanged himself in one of the rooms, but no one at the hotel told that to the guests assigned to that room!

Mary's grandfather, Joe Vergolio, had migrated to this country when barely 16 years old, coming over with an uncle. This new country didn't have streets of gold, and the uncle, taking with him all the funds both had, abandoned young Joe and shipped back to Italy. Joe, speaking no English, did what he could to stay alive and gradually worked his way west to Cerrillos. It was some time before he had enough gold dust to buy the Palace from the Green family, who had built it, but he paid for it and promptly put in a vineyard and fruit trees surrounding the back part of the big lot.

Mary's father ran a grocery store while his wife ran the hotel, and the children went across the big bridge to school on the other

FIRE BLACKENED ruins of famous old hotel.

OLD HOTEL before fire destroyed it several years ago.

4

side of the river. That bridge was washed out twice, and the second time it was not rebuilt, but the concrete and stone abutment, partially covered with weeds, still mutely testifies that it once spanned the river. Cerrillos seemed fated to have too little water or too much — for one of the floods coming down washed away seven houses.

Mary remembers the old church, the one before the present one, and the sky blue oilcloth ceiling which she thought the most beautiful thing in the whole world. The priest came for services from far away Peña Blanca, and since horseback was his means of transportation when he came, he stayed with parisioners over night. When the present church was built, a room was built especially for the priest to have a place of his own. That was in 1922.

The old schoolhouse across the river still stands, " . . . but they took off the second story," Mary mourns. She grew up and became a teacher, teaching in Golden, Galisteo and in her home town of Cerrillos before her own soldier boy, Leo Mora, returned from a German prison camp.

Traveling around Cerrillos with Mary Mora is a real treat, for she remembers so very much. Even the cemetery brings up memories. She paused at one headstone and told us of a young wife with an adored son and a husband who gave her little of his time. The child died, and the young mother turned to another man for comfort and affection. Plans were made to run away with him and, when he didn't come at the appointed time, the woman put on her wedding dress and shot herself. The husband buried her

OUTSKIRTS OF CERRILLOS.

next to her child and then he, too, left never to return. The other man was not seen around Cerrillos again, not even for the funeral.

"Your grandfather was a wonderful man," she smiles at Marsha Zucal. "He had the saloon which is now called Tiffany's, which was a grocery store and had farming equipment and a lot of other things too then. You know, of course, that your doctor father (Dr. Louis Zucal) was born and grew up here in Cerrillos.

"One night three men held up your grandfather's place and he dived through a window, getting a bad cut on his throat. He had the scar from that cut until he died. He knew that they meant to kill him, and he wasn't about to stand still and give them the chance to do it easily! He was really a wonderful man!"

"Not all the men who came to Cerrillos were his kind. There was always somebody getting shot or sliced up with a knife. The darndest thing was when one shot killed two people! Two men were having a fight, and one pulled out a pistol and shot the other. The bullet went through the first man and hit another man just back of him. The second man lived a short while, but finally died of the wound."

Cerrillos is quite a movie set these days, for they don't have to build sets. The false front stores, wooden sidewalks and dirt roads are just as they once were. A few individuals gripe about having to get their cars or trucks out of sight when a film is being "shot," but mostly they pay little attention. Most of the old homes have returned to the adobe soil from which they sprang, but there are still a few, and "too darned many hippies" some of the residents say. Mitchell, a former Santa Fe school teacher, has a most amusing "What Not" shop that finds a sells memorabilia of the old days from cut glass to gem stones, sadirons to Indian pots — it's better than a museum.

The population that was once 4,000 is now around 100. Of all the mines — Mina del Tierra, Little Joe, Darling, Nick-O-Time and many others — only Cash Entry is still extant. Of the many homes that surrounded this mine, about three miles up the canyon from Cerrillos, only one lovely old brick house remains, and it is filled with equipment once used in retrieving metal — plus a plethora of "No Trespassing" signs. Tipples and sheds still exist there, and it is wired for electricity.

The golden days are over, but Cerrillos is a wonderful little town to visit and to see a "mellerdrama" in the old Pat Hogan saloon and make all sorts of discoveries for yourself.

6

II.

The Traps

Las Trampas

Many tourists from all over the world journey to New York to see the Statue of Liberty. Many New Yorkers haven't bothered. It's there, they know that, but they are busy, uninterested, or only well-meaning. Someday they will, the plan, but someday stays in the future.

Far too many of us emulate the New Yorker. We have such beautiful scenery, quaint villages, old world charm with hospitality that is hard to match. Even the people in the villages sometimes forget what beauty they have. At a mountain village, Las Trampas, they had looked at their church, San Jose de Gracia de Las Trampas, so long (all their lives) that in reality they no longer saw it. Only when the things of our youth are gone are they mourned and appreciated — and this was almost the experience of the villagers in Las Trampas.

Until the highway (or high road to Taos) was put in, the people of Las Trampas were almost as isolated as they had been in 1751 when 74-year-old Juan de Arguello took with him a dozen families and settled here among the tall pine and spruce to found a Spanish outpost. This happened at a time when danger of roving Indian bands terrorized even the older, established villages such as Taos, Don Fernando de Taos, Picuris and Santa Cruz. Comanches, Apaches, Utes and, occasionally, Navajo raiding parties found that raiding the villages for their stores of grain, cattle, sheep and sometimes the people themselves for use as slaves was lucrative. Spanish colonial policy forbad giving the settlers guns and ammunition, even to protect themselves, much less as a means of supplying themselves with food in the form of wild game that roamed the forests and often dined on their fields of grain, beans and squash. Authorities did want the settlements, for they provided a buffer zone for the more populous areas such as Santa Cruz, but some of their policies made life in remote villages even more arduous than it would normally have been.

7

SAN JOSE DE GRACIA DE LAS TRAMPAS.

Why Arguello, at his advanced age, would consider leaving his Santa Fe home of over 40 years to lead this group is a mystery. Men in their 70's rarely look for new worlds to conquer, or persuade daughters and their husbands to go with them, but he did. They all went, including Sebastian Rodriguez, an African drummer boy who had come in with De Vargas, and they built their homes in a tight square around a plaza, the safest way possible during this early day as evidenced by not only other villages, but even by the capital city itself, Santa Fe.

Spaniards of an early day were very religious, and the closest church to Trampas was nine miles away at Picuris. The people of Trampas wanted their own church, and there was only one way to have it — build it themselves. Despite their meagre, hard-earned crop yields, one-sixth was set aside for the chapel, including the efforts of laboring with their own hands. Women mixed adobe and plastered, fed the men who slowly raised the four-foot-thick walls, and strained to put the vigas in place. They labored well, for the church stands today much as it was when they built it. Sometimes it is called the Church of the Twelve Apostles, recalling not only the Biblical 12 apostles, but the 12 men who did a great deal of the original work, as well.

By the time the village was 16 years old, the original dozen families had grown to 63. But, today it is, as most of the villages are, dying. Only 34 families own land there today — and some of these owners no longer live in the village.

Las Trampas could not have a resident priest — there simply were not enough to supply the demand — but they did have the close-knit brotherhood called the Penitentes. The small adobe building huddled close against the back of the church is said to be their *morada*. Someone once said that there are no atheists in foxholes. In early days, these little villages were, in a manner of speaking, foxholes, for the people were often in danger and no help was available save in their faith. The Penitente brotherhood kept the faith alive, and not only that, but out of their zeal grew the only American-born art form not extant when the Spaniard arrived. Their *santos* and *bultos* were fashioned from the wood that grew around them, coated with *yeso* and painted with vegetable dyes laboriously gathered from the fields and mountains, with pulverized clays and rock and with black from the charcoal of their hearth fires. Far too little credit has been given these dedicated men and their contributions to the colonization of New Mexico.

In the name of "progress," New Mexico, and the world, almost lost the beautiful old church at Trampas only a few years ago.

A highway, needed by the peoples in the isolated villages, was being planned. When the engineers surveyed through Las Trampas, the new highway would destroy the churchyard and be within six feet of the church itself. With all the space around Las Trampas, surely this need not be done.

Nathaniel A. Owings, nationally recognized architect and writer, keeps not only a home at Nambe, but carries in his heart a love of New Mexico and our cultural heritage wherever he goes. A clip from *The New Mexican* about the danger to the plaza and the church at Las Trampas sent to him in Washington by a Nambe

neighbor. In Santa Fe, John Gaw Meem and John McHugh appealed to Gov. Jack Campbell, while Owings worked on the historic sites committees and other influential people in Washington. Urgency, speed, had to be exercised, for the highway routing was not announced until they were ready to proceed with the work. Owings worked so swiftly, backed by interested Santa Feans, that Las Trampas became "the only case of an instant historic landmark designation on record."

The highway was rerouted and handled in such a way that it impinges but little on the feeling and authenticity of the village. Not people to do a half job, the men who had worked

DETAIL of churchyard gate.

10

so hard to save the church now worked just as hard to restore it where time had taken its toll. Today the church is visited by many, for its beauty is nonpareil.

The wide plank flooring is still there, the painted *vigas* and corbels still sturdy. Doña Sebastiana, the skeleton figure in the death cart that for many years stood in the room to the right of the entrance, is no longer there. The caretaker could not, or possibly would not, tell us where she is now, but it is to be hoped she is safely guarded and taken care of.

Lighting in the church is still provided by candles in prim rows on cross bars raised and lowered by ropes. The old bell, called Refugio, is safely in the bell tower. It is one of a pair, the one used to announce solemn events. The companion bell, called Gracia, was of a higher tone and was used to announce feast days, weddings and lesser occasions. It was stolen in 1909 and has never been replaced.

Residents take turns as keeper of the keys. The church is locked, but those wanting to inspect the interior can easily ascertain who the keeper is this month and find them gracious, hospitable and kindly. The plaza is unkempt, buildings around it

PLAZA at Las Trampas showing old schoolhouse at right.

huddled like ancient monks saying their beads. Some are occupied, some are not.

Las Trampas – the traps – has trapped 200 years of beauty and calm.

LOG FLUME still brings water across canyon to irrigate fields in the valley.

NORBERTO VIGIL, village patriarch.

III.

Round Hill of the Little Bells

Cundiyo

Knock on any door in the little village of Cundiyo and ask "Is this the Vigil home?" The answer is always yes, for the entire population of 25 families carries the name Vigil. What's more, they are all related, either by blood or marriage. Indeed, the village is often called *Los Vigiles.*

Cundiyo, "the round hill of the little bells" as it was named by the Tewa Indians, rides the ridge at the confluence of the Rio Medio and the Rio Frijoles. This spot was chosen by a common ancestor, Capt. Jose Antonio Vigil, who exercised his right as a soldier to be given a land grant when his service in the Army was completed. He was stationed at nearby Santa Cruz before the American occupation and perhaps saw this locale while chasing raiding Comanches or Apaches or even while hunting for stray horses. The ridge was chosen as a home site because such a location was more easily defended than the valleys below.

When he died, the land went to his five sons. It has been

13

ROUGH STEPS, several generations old, were made from cedar logs and flagstone.

divided by inheritance many times since then, but always it is the property of a Vigil. The boys find wives in nearby villages and build their homes here. The girls go out into other places with their husbands, but the male line stays put remarkably well.

The patriarch of the village now is more than 80 years old. He is twinkle-eyed Norberto Vigil. He still carries on his share of caring for the irrigation ditches and farming during the summer months, since the Vigils have purchased land outside the grant for grazing and growing grain. He also weaves on the big handmade looms during cold weather. It was his wife, Elena, who brought weaving to Cundiyo, bringing her own loom with her when they were married over 60 years ago at Chimayo. Now most families in the village have looms, and both men and women weave to supplement cash crop income. Ready market for weaving is found in Chimayo, for this distinctive type of weaving has become renowned for excellence, originality and beauty. Norberto and Elena are both master weavers.

Noberto, growing up in Cundiyo, had no formal schooling until he was in his teens when the first schoolmaster came to the village. He had been taught to write with a stick in a smoothed out, sandy place as he and his father watched the sheep, so that he was able to do three grades a year when formal schooling began.

It was quite a change from his pre-teen years when he often spent weeks with a cousin companion herding sheep in the mountains. His first cash earning was for bounty on three mountain lions which made the mistake of trying to make a meal on the sheep he was caring for. That was when he was eight or nine years old. He hated the lions anyway and had already killed one when a second one showed up.

"My teeth were very noisy," he admits, laughing. "When the second one came out of the rocks I killed him too, but didn't have any bullets left for my gun. Then there was another one! I sent my cousin back to Cundiyo to get help and built a fire while I waited for my father to come. Lions don't like fires, and I stayed very close to the fire. I was very hungry so I roasted some of the first lion to eat. The third lion did not come down, you bet! He stayed up in the rocks. My father let me shoot him when he came with bullets for the gun."

It was a proud boy who climbed up on the wagon seat later to take the hides to Santa Fe and collect the bounty. It took two full days to go, and two more to come back, but he had six dollars in real money when he returned.

Norberto worked with the Forest Service and helped bring the first telephone line into the village and Forest Service headquarters there. After his service in the Army (World War I in France), he

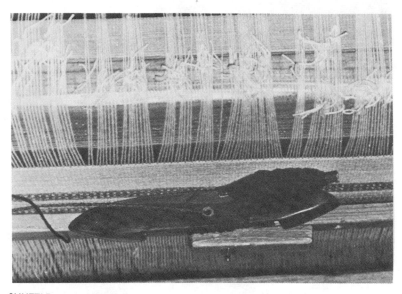

SHUTTLE carved from pear wood rests in loom.

returned to Cundiyo, married and, as a responsible family man, circulated the petition for a post office. They got it, and he was made first postmaster (1922). The post office occupied one corner in his little grocery store which had been set up in one room of their home. After 12 years he needed more time to farm, and Mrs. Vigil became postmaster, a position she held for 30 years, making this family hold that office for 42 years. She retired several years ago.

Norberto, who has a keen sense of humor, always finds something to laugh at in any situation. Several years back, a team of young students from India was sent to Cundiyo to study village life and farming methods. They stayed with Norberto and his wife.

"They were nice boys, but they know nothing of farming," he says. "They were *ricos* (rich). How could I show them how to do things differently when they didn't know how it was done in their own country? 'What do you eat?' one asked me when his belt was already too tight from eating the good supper Elena had fixed. I don't know where he put all the food he ate, so I laugh and say, 'Oh! we eat everything — snakes, lizards, rats, weeds. Didn't you like?' Elena shakes her head, mad with me, and that boy, he doesn't know what to say to me.

"Another one asks me why everyone is named Vigil, so I tell him and then he asks, 'If a girl marries someone and comes back to

16

live here, her name will not be Vigil, no?' I laugh some more and point to that big cottonwood tree down there," he motions toward a stately old tree. "If his name not Vigil in two weeks, we just hang him on that tree."

The next morning, very early, the boys announced they had some business in Santa Fe, and away they went and did not return. Norberto was not angry, only amused.

The Norberto Vigils had four daughters and one son. The son was killed by lightning while in the Army, stationed at Fort Bliss. Two of the girls (all are college-trained) are teachers, while Adelina followed her father in working for the Forest Service. They all go home to visit at every opportunity.

The village now has one store (the Norberto Vigils have closed theirs) which also dispenses gasoline; three churches, with only one in use. Many of their young folks work in Española, Los Alamos or Santa Fe. No help of any kind is hired in the village, but they do help each other. If a field is to be threshed, several of the men will show up to help. Their turn to be helped will come next week! Homes are neat and well maintained, and TV antennas have to climb high into the air to catch the invisible waves that bring them New York or Hollywood.

No longer do they have to fear Indian raids, and homes have spilled down the hillsides, but not into the rich bottom land that is saved for the growing of crops. Fruit trees are scattered wherever there is room to let one find soil for its roots. Flowers grow

BARN at side of highway.

17

around the houses and border kitchen garden spots. Potted geraniums and other flowering plants grace the deep window sills. Corner fireplaces still bring the family together in the evening to pop corn, roast marshmallows, etc., while the *abuelos* (grandparents) tell the children stories from their own youth or those they learned from their parents in front of the same fireplace.

The land has been divided so many times through the generations that no one individual owns much, but it is still all Vigil owned. If an inheritor wants to sell his share, there is always a Vigil willing and anxious to buy, for this is, and will remain, the village of the Vigils. It isn't LIKE one big family — it IS one big family which gets along well together and with the world outside.

IV.

Cimarron

In southwestern usage "Cimarron" means a wild or unruly person or untamed animal. The village of Cimarron did its collective best in early days to live up to its name. As villages go in New Mexico, it was relatively late in getting started, despite its plentiful water, game, timber, rich soil and beauty. Utes and Apaches looked upon this area as their own game preserve and stomping ground, and they violently discouraged the white-eyes.

The 1841 filing of the Beaubien and Miranda Grant made the territory personal property, so that when Lucien B. Maxwell married Luz, the 15-year-old daughter of Judge Beaubien, it was natural for them to establish a home ranch. They first built a house at Rayado, then, for reasons of safety and better trading potential, moved to Cimarron and built a "palace" of a home there. This house was in two parts, the front part being used as business and quarters for male guests. Across the patio were the kitchens, women's quarters and storerooms. A ten-foot wall guarded the patio from outside view. These houses, containing at least 39 and in some reports up to 50 rooms, eventually burned, so that nothing remains of them today.

GRISTMILL built by Maxwell, today a museum.

There are those who say that the burning of the Maxwell house was arson, for fire started there not once, but twice. The second time proved fatal for the structure. It was the center of the Colfax County War, after all. Maxwell had sold out, gone to Fort Sumner, but the old mansion was headquarters for the Dutch firm that had bought him out.

Visitors today stop for lunch or to stay overnight in Cimarron along the highway. That isn't old Cimarron. The old Cimarron town plaza (who ever heard of a village without a plaza?) today stands weed-grown and neglected just off the old road to Taos. An

HOLLOWED OUT log flume at Clear Creek where Tolby met death.

TOMBSTONE of Rev. F. J. Tolby.

ancient well in the middle marks the site. A Cimarron doctor has built a very lovely home on the site of the Maxwell house. Older than the Don Diego Hotel, the National Hotel, is trim, tidy and cared for and about. The "Webster Girls," stepdaughters of Springer, live in the National and care for it lovingly and carefully. It is painted in gay colors. The floors, though wide planking pegged down, have been sanded and waxed, and the building itself is beautiful. It has no bullet holes, no record of murders, no echoes of rowdy fights, for it never had a bar. It was a family hotel, a place where a man could take his wife and children and be assured that they were safe and well-treated.

One old house, woebegone and slattern with age, stands on the far side of the old plaza. Next door there is only a pile of debris and rusted, abandoned cars to mark where the Grant-owned printing press was thrown into the river. W.R. Morley was at that time manager of the Grant. He went on to earn kudos as the man who surveyed Raton Pass for the Santa Fe Railroad, won a wild horseback race against a train to the Royal Gorge and finally died from an accidental shotgun blast while surveying in Mexico. While Grant manager, he lived in the Maxwell house in Cimarron, and it was in this house that his daughter, Agnes Morley Cleaveland, was born. She became not only a leader down Datil way, in the southern part of the state, but an author of repute and standing. Her son, Norman, after a long career in engineering, also is a writer.

By the side of the road (now the road leading to Philmont Boy Scout Ranch) a block off the old Plaza, stands Swink's Saloon, gambling house, cafe, dance hall, what have you. It is plaqued as an historic site, and now serves as a residence. As a residence it is unusual, of course. In what other home could one find a kitchen drainboard of marble, one with a dark stain in one corner? This stain is, according to legend, from the blood of a buffalo soldier (Negro), purportedly killed by Clay Allison. Again, the house has that rare phenomena we call a ghost the ghost of one Mr. Garcia who was murdered in this house. He locks doors if the tenants forget to do it when leaving the house, but the ghost of a red-haired woman, discovered buried beneath the floor, does not share his nocturnal walks. No one knows anything about the woman, for no such person was ever reported as missing in Cimarron police records.

Cimarron was a natural rest stop on the Taos branch of the Santa Fe Trail. It was also a center for dispersing of commodities as treaties were made with the Indians. Maxwell built a large, three-

PHILMONT Scout Ranch, the former residence of Waite Phillips.

21

OLD NATIONAL HOTEL.

story grist mill that remains as a monument to him and his endeavors. It is now being used as a museum and is well worth visiting. This mill served as headquarters for the Indian Agency from 1870 to 1878. Fred Lambert, son of Henri, was curator here until his death a few years ago.

Speaking of monuments, there is a statue of Maxwell, painted anew each year, in the new town plaza. It depicts Maxwell seated with a gun across his lap. It is so bad as sculpture that it's good. The visitor will remember it in its gaucheness better than he will remember a really good piece of art.

For the romantically inclined. the secret wedding of Maxwell's daughter, Virigina, to Capt. A.S.B. Keyes took place on the third floor of the mill. Maxwell was opposed to the match, and Virginia failed in her effort to get a young French priest then in Cimarron to read the vows. The priest was afraid of Papa Maxwell's wrath. She was more successful with Reverend Thomas Harwood, a Methodist circuit missionary, and Virginia and Keyes were married on March 30, 1870, while Maxwell was distributing supplies to the Indians. He eventually forgave both the couple and the circuit rider whom he had threatened to whip on sight. Forgiveness did take a long time, though.

It was inevitable that a village would grow around the Maxwell holdings in Cimarron. Maxwell himself became the first postmaster in 1861.

Cowpokes all over northern New Mexico made Cimarron their

22

target. Some were high-spirited, shooting their guns into the air when they became overheated with Taos "lightning." Some were not merely high-spirited but were often dangerous. Clay Allison, of whom fact has so mingled with legend that a true picture becomes almost impossible, had a spread in the Cimarron area. He was prone to go for his guns when liquored up, and his guns were deadly. He also liked his liquor, so periods of disorder were frequent.

Barroom fights were common and often fatal, sometimes starting over card games or personal slights, however negligible. There were 11 deaths of this type in one barroom in one month!

Meanwhile, gold had been discovered in E'town (Elizabethtown), and there was a great influx of gold hunters. Among them was Henri Lambert who had been a chef for Lincoln. He soon decided that there was more gold to be earned with a frying pan than a gold pan. He opened a hotel, the St. James, in Cimarron. It was successful, and many famous people of the period were guests — Kit Carson and Buffalo Bill (who was staying at the St. James the night Fred Lambert was born) were but a couple. The old St. James still stands, renamed the Don Diego, and accepts guests as well as sponsoring guided tours through the old hostelry.

After Maxwell sold the Grant and the Dutch owners had put Morley in as manager, they ran a newspaper here. A great deal of dissention had come up relative to "squatters" and others who felt honestly entitled to the Grant land they had perhaps purchased in good faith or had just settled on. Feelings ran high with uninvolved people taking sides. The press on which the newspaper was printed was once dumped into the river with Clay Allison taking part in the dumping. The next day, sober, he gave Mrs. Morley money to buy a new press.

Rev. Thomas Tolby, a Methodist minister who served E'town and Cimarron, was loudly outspoken against leaders on both the Grant and anti-Grant sides. In 1875 his body was found near Clear Creek in Cimarron Canyon. He had been murdered. Vigilantes picked on one Cruz Vega and hanged him, but that didn't settle the matter. No one was sure why Tolby had been murdered any more than who had done it. Nothing to date has been uncovered to throughly substantiate any single version of the killing.

The unruly village of Cimarron today looks rather nondescript unless one pauses long enough to get off the highway, see and listen a little. A clod kicked over is a part of history that is now a tamed village. A visit to the cemetery is like reading the pages of the past incised into stone — the good and bad men buried side by each other.

Just out of village limits is the national Boy Scout ranch which became the property of the Scouts as a gift from Waite Phillips who had built a magnificent ranch home here in the hills above the valley. Thousands of visitors each year come to Cimarron as Scouts or to visit the Scout ranch which has a great deal of interest to show.

Orchards, fat cattle, saw mills, thriving little businesses make the village seem average. It was never that, nor will the people there ever feel it is that today, for they remember "the good old days" when those who survived to tell about it all were the good guys.

V.

El Rito

"El Rito," said the late Tom Martin, "is a happy place. We could use some more people now, people who want to put down roots, to live here and take part in the community and for the community." Tom Martin should know, for this had been his home all his life. The Martin family came to El Rito in 1910, when George Martin, Tom's father, was brought in from the east as the first president of the new Normal School.

Happy places are hard to find in history books, which tend to chronicle the violent, the unhappy, the tragic, even as newspapers today write little of the quiet lives of people but center on robberies, rapes, controversy in all its aspects. People read about misfortune far more readily than they do about the unspectacular lives of the ordinary citizen. So, El Rito is mentioned in Twitchell's five-volume "History of New Mexico" only once as the site of the Normal School. It was, and is, a quiet, agricultural community.

The school has changed objectives several times and is now a vocational and technical training center for northern New Mexico.

BEAUTY of such old homes inspired Roberta Martin Brosseau to become a serious student of painting.

25

OLD SARGENT HOUSE now occupied by Mr. Procter with a quilt making project.

FIRE, the scourge of any village, took the life of this old home.

The Martin boys all attended El Rito, but their one daughter, Roberta, was sent down to Loretto Academy in Santa Fe. They think highly of the school, which during one straight academic period included two years of college.

George Martin was a bachelor when he came west, but lost his heart twice over — first to the pretty community nurse (who had been the first anesthetist at St. Vincent Hospital in Santa Fe) and secondly to the countryside. He never left the country, though he did leave education for business. He and John Sargent became partners in a general merchandise store that carried everything from collar buttons to coffins, baking powder to buggies. That store burned, and although the family does not dwell on the event, Dr. Molly Radford Martin (unrelated), in her book about her husband's career as a state policeman and detective, gives a very interesting account of this period in El Rito and of the fire, which was, she says, deliberately set.

The Tierra Amarilla trouble of the 1960's was not the first of the land grant troubles in Rio Arriba County. This had been Spanish-American territory and some of the grants were ill defined. After the coming of the Anglo, bits and pieces of the land were purchased by the newcomers — some of it land that had been community grazing land for generations and some of it land sold for taxes. A number of secret organizations proliferated all over northern New Mexico, and there was one called Mano Negro (Black Hand) or more often "The Night Riders." They were really an organized ring of thieves, stealing sheep, horses, household goods, and were excellent at burning haystacks, barns and even homes. The native population was terrified of them, for they, too, were victims, and brutal beatings or murder followed any report to authorities.

Policeman Martin succeeded in tracing down and arresting the son of a rival grocer in the Sargent-Martin fire and in getting him and several others jailed for various forays. The repentent convicted arsonist later made beaded belts for grocer Martin and his four sons.

Sheep raising was one of the major industries in El Rito, and, after the railroad reached La Madera, wool and hides were shipped out from there. The Martins also bought flour sacks full of pinon nuts and shipped them to Gross Kelly who in turn marketed them in the east.

Sheep were often trailed to Navajo Country for the winter because of generous snowfalls that blanketed the fields of El Rito and covered the graze. It was at El Rito that one of the first (if not the very first) ski runs was put in, with the Forest Service and CCC Camps constructing the tow lines and runs. Roberta Martin

Brosseau has some nice old pictures of that activity.

Hunting has always been good in the El Rito district, and a great guest ranch was put in with hunters coming in from all over the country for the hunting of deer, bear, elk and other game, adding fishing during the summer months. This once guest ranch is now owned by Mrs. Felicity Wilson.

The river was much higher years ago than it is now. Tom Martin could recall when the fishing limit was 100, then dropped to 50, and he could ride out in the morning and return after lunch with his limit of native trout.

El Rito, like most of the mountain villages, is losing population. There are so few jobs for the young people. The two grist mills, one above and one below town, have long since disappeared. Charles Procter has a quilt-making business there now, while Michael Parker specializes in hand dipped and molded decorative candles. Peter van Dresser has a coffee shop which closes during the winter months. He grows organic food for use in his charming little place. He also is a writer. El Rito is a nice place for a writer! Peaceful, friendly, quiet.

Big (by village standards) houses line the one main street and speak of a day when a good farmer or sheepman could make a more than adequate living for his family. That day has passed.

The trees grow tall and thick around the homes so that it is difficult to really see them until frost has scattered their leafy green. The Catholic Church in El Rito was built in 1832 (the date is carved into a great beam), and there also is a Protestant church, both in main El Rito. Another part of town, called lower El Rito

DESERTED CHURCH in lower El Rito.

28

or Las Placitas, boasts one store, two churches and a few houses, besides the fire-blackened ruin of what must have been a lovely home.

Roberta Martin Brosseau and Ernestine Evans (so long New Mexico's Secretary of State) are both El Rito natives. The lovely old Jaramillo house (now owned by Patrick Martin) is where author Cleofas Jaramilllo went as a bride.

Mrs. Brosseau loves the old home town and treasures old pictures as well as memories. She may someday write about it — we devoutely hope so, for El Rito is such a nice little village, and she is the one who can tell its story, for the Martin family had a great part in the development of El Rito.

The dream that someone once had of making El Rito a railroad center never came to pass, but Peter van Dresser has the original typescript of the plan to do just that. Perhaps it is just as well, for a railroad yard just might have destroyed part of the charm that is El Rito today.

DESCANSO, resting place for funeral processions before days of motorized hearses. Each cross signifies that a coffin was placed at the site while coffin bearers rested, prayed and meditated on the way to the cemetery.

VI.
San Buenaventura de Chimayo

Chimayo is a Spanish village, and a mood. If this mood of serenity, brotherhood, could be bottled and sold, the village would be innundated (and destroyed) by outlanders seeking to buy and carry away that which is Chimayo. During the summer, tour buses and cars crowd the roads and cameras click endlessly. Sometimes, back home, these tourists can snatch a bit of the memory and sigh regretfully that they could not have had more time here.

There is no hotel, no golf course, and only one place to get a meal — Arturo Jaramillo's restaurant, occupying one of the old houses built by twin brothers on opposite sides of the narrow valley. The Jaramillo family lives in one and operates a restaurant and cocktail lounge in the other, wisely keeping the old atmosphere and hospitality that is inborn in the villagers — wide, pegged-board flooring, santo niches (niches for favorite family saints), handmade furniture, drapes and upholstery woven by their old friends, the Ortegas. The restaurant sits back on a hillside, the road passing through the orchard — old, but still bearing fruit.

Few of the tourists ever see the old plaza of Chimayo, built tight in a square for protection, for life in the early villages existed only through eternal vigilance. The middle of the plaza today is given over to the growing of corn and chili, the chili that New Mexicans love above all others for its flavor.

Narrow openings between the houses brought in the accquias,

31

MODEL CHURCH sits on wall at the Church of Santo Niño.

irrigation ditches, and it is here that the old *oratorio* the family chapel of the Ortega family, still stands. Unfortunately, Satan-inspired thieves only a few years ago stole the old *santos* from the chapel along with the sweetest sounding bell in all the southwest. Those who believe that justice must and will prevail know that someday, somehow, the *santos* and bell will return. Perhaps the old store on the plaza may once again open its doors. For years after it closed, the remaining merchandise in this old store was dusted carefully each week, but now the shelves are clean and bare.

The Ortega family, weavers for six generations, have a quite modern store and a weaving room a couple of blocks away, up near the highway. Not only are all the family weavers, but they function as contractors for weaving, and a market for weavers. Frequently, the Ortegas furnish yarn for weaving to homes up and down the valley and when the weaving is done, it is brought back to the Ortegas and the homebound weavers are paid for their work. Few families are there where the handmade looms do not occupy space in adobe homes, with weaving from 12 to 54 inches wide, and these looms are a precious heritage. In the winter months, pause by almost any snug adobe home and listen and you'll hear the soft thump as mothers, fathers, children "walk'. the looms. David Ortega helped one man, badly injured in an accident, to construct a loom he could "walk" from his wheelchair. This spirit of helping, too, is an integral part of Chimayo.

Rugs, drapery, purses, capes, coats are fashioned by the Ortegas and their faithful weavers (about 65 of them now) and though Chimayo weaving never wears out, they cannot meet the demand. They have no salesmen out "on the road," but orders come in from all over the world, for Chimayo weaving is unique. From the Vatican to Franklin D. Roosevelt, as well as all over the southwest, their weaving has been a prized possession among people who know good craftsmanship and love beauty. Special orders are woven, but in main the weavers, in the argot of the day, "do their own thing."

Chimayo was the eastern boundary of Nuevo Méjico from 1598 to 1695, and visiting this village today is walking back into that time without its dangers. Building on the site of an old Tewa Pueblo, the original settlers may have learned at least some of their weaving techniques from the Indians. Adding to this, if indeed it was there, the Bazan brothers, Ignacio and Juan, expert weavers, were sent to New Mexico to teach weaving in 1805. They didn't like Santa Fe, but they did like Chimayo, and they settled in this little village. Undoubtedly, they contributed much. Weaving was mostly confined to doing for one's own family until Nacacio Ortega began organizing and marketing the unique product of their looms. He was himself a master weaver, and when hard times hit the valley (as such periods are experienced everywhere), it was he who loaded weaving into his wagon and went out away from the village to sell Chimayo's unique product. Word of mouth kept it going, and still does.

The old Sanctuario chapel, built by Don Bernardo Abeyta in 1816, is more than a tourist attraction. This twin-towered old church is the Fatima or Lourdes of the United States, for in one tiny room at the left of the altar is the healing dirt. A hole in the dirt floor yields healing for the ills of the many who come to it with faith and prayer. The ante-room is filled with crutches, braces, etc., where the afflicted hobbled in only to walk out with no longer any need of them. The hole never grows larger, though thousands have taken small quanities of the dirt for self, or carried it back home to isolated ranchos in case of sudden illness in the family, or to allay a mountain storm with a few grains thrown into the fireplace.

Sanctuario was a family chapel until 1929 when old art treasures in the chapel were put on sale. Writer Mary Austin was instrumental in securing money from an anonymous donor to repurchase these treasures and

YOUNGEST of the famed Ortega family is skillful weaver.

ARTURO JARAMILLO home, Chimayo. Window on end is made from two single windows, and people came for miles to see "the big windows" when the home was first built.

the building itself, which was turned over to the Roman Catholic Church. It is open for visitors, and often, on the lone road to Chimayo, people will be seen walking, fulfilling a vow or seeking healing. When the remnants of New Mexico's 200th returned from Japan after the fall of Corregidor, they marched from Santa Fe to Chimayo to kneel and give thanks for their deliverance.

Nearby is the privately owned church of Santo Niño, and both churches claim their own Santo Niño travels up and down the valley during the night hours to soothe the restless child, heal the ill, comfort the grieving. A special gift is that of tiny shoes for the Santo Nino, for his shoes are worn out frequently. A new church, very modern looking, has been built in the village, but it does not engender the same type of love given to El Sanctuario. How could it? It is new, while the old chapel has been a part of the lives of the people for so long. Once two great cottonwoods guarded the gateway to El Sanctuario, but now one is gone, a victim of age. The second one remains. Many New Mexicans mourn the old tree that is gone, for it was a part of the scene painted by so many artists, so lovely as a framework of green for the first sight of the chapel.

High on the hills here and in the surrounding area are tiny private chapels, attesting to the religious fervor of the faithful.

Many of the old adobe houses are in a state of ruin, but in the spring wild plum bushes scent the air, mixed with the odor of blossoming fruit trees and roses climbing over walls, hiding the scars of time and adding their beauty to the old village.

An old *descanso* — resting place for funeral processions — rarely have a new cross added now, and many of the old ones have fallen. Staghorn cactus has proliferated among the crosses, first put in during the time when caskets were carried by friends to the *camposanto* (cemetery). They lowered the casket at intervals, rested, prayed for the departed and meditated. Wherever such a procession stopped, a wooden cross was erected. Sometimes, in this day of motorized hearses, an old resident will request that the funeral procession pause at the *descanso* and when this is done, a new wooden cross is erected.

Sometimes the tourist sees small charcoal and ash heaps around the churches and along the road. These are the remains of *luminarias* (or *farolitas*) lighted to guide the Holy Child and his worshippers for a special Saint's day celebration. During December they appear more frequently.

Chimayo manages to maintain its identity, charm and serenity despite a modern highway cutting through the village. The homes all have gardens gay with flowers, and hollyhocks (the staff of St. Joseph which blossomed when he was chosen as spouse for Mary) bloom extravagantly against adobe walls and along ancient water-ways. Chimayo is a wise man's dream solidified in time and beauty.

OLD STORE on the original plaza.

SMALL GIRL of yesterday stands between yesteryear's method of refrigeration — huge blocks of ice. *(Museum of New Mexico Photo)*

VII.

Lamy

The steam steed, guided by reins of steel, tossed its smoky mane in the mountain winds and whistled premonitorially for the men who served it. In New Mexico in the 1880s, they came quickly and gladly, for the steam engine was Progress. It stopped often for the tribute of black diamonds and clear waters, and where it stopped towns grew up. In 1879 one of these new towns was Galisteo Junction.

The Santa Fe Railroad had slowly followed the old wagon train route over the miles of countryside, and at this point a decision had to be made. The Ancient City of the Holy Faith was no longer the end of the trail — there was "Californy" and the far, far west beckoning on.

Galisteo Junction was a bit larger than most of the towns along the railroad. The big wheels of the locomotives were geared for speed on level tracks, but slipped and spun despite all the sand poured on the rails to help them when steep grades had to be climbed. Smaller wheeled engines had to be kept corraled and ready to help, and here the glistening black behemoths had to be pushed over nearby Glorieta Pass.

The decision was made to head for Albuquerque, to by-pass the goal carried in the name of the railroad itself. The City of Santa Fe was not happy, for they wanted the railroad.

Archbishop John B. Lamy was not only a religious leader, but an indefatigable civic worker. It was he who, while accepting the expanded vision of the railroad officials, spearheaded the move to put in a spur track to Santa Fe with the city to pay for it. The cost was high, but the $150,000 bond issued carried 3-1, only 18 votes being cast against it in Santa Fe proper, and the spur was built. While in main the spur was used for freight, a passenger coach did run on this spur at one time. C.C. Robinson, genial railroad agent at Lamy, remembered riding it in 1917. He was then a relief operator at Lamy. Certainly the existence of the spur was a vital factor in the establishment of Bruns General Hospital in Santa Fe in the 1940s.

The exact reason for the change of name from Galisteo Junction to Lamy is not known. It could have been the too close existence of Galisteo, or it could have been a gesture of tribute to the man who had worked so hard for the spur. The change of name did, however, become effective January 6, 1881.

The town grew. Fred Harvey sent in a dining car from Las Vegas in 1881, and served meals continuously from then on, eventually building the Lamy Harvey House, the quaint and lovely El Ortiz, which was highly popular not only with train passengers and crews, but with the countryside as far away as Santa Fe.

The railroad brought in people, the great and not so desirable. The railroad recruited settlers from the more populous east and brought them to develop the new frontier. Two hotels soon followed the two boarding houses and a church was built. A post office, that official accolade of a prospering frontier town's importance, was opened March 1, 1881, with Daniel A. Phillips as postmaster, only to be mysteriously closed on July 13 and re-established as of February 8, 1884, with John Stein as postmaster.

Brushing elbows with the first respectable citizens debarking at Lamy was a bunco ring, fleecing the unwary with guile, while armed robberies and murder were not unknown. The six gun could be used for other purposes than protection from snakes! The saloon also did a land office business, literally and figuratively.

By 1889 the population had reached 100. A stone quarry was in operation and furnished the stone for the building of the state capitol building. Long strings of burros plodded in from the hills laden with wood for the charcoal ovens that flourished and furnished charcoal for use as far away as San Francisco's Chinatown.

CHARCOAL OVENS at Lamy once provided charcoal as far away as San Francisco. (Museum of New Mexico Photo)

EL ORTIZ Harvey House at Lamy years ago. *(Museum of New Mexico Photo)*

Wood cutters, herders, roundhouse men watched the trains come in and saw such personages as Gen. U.S. Grant, Rutherford B. Hayes, Sheridan, Sherman and Rough Rider Roosevelt climb down to take the stage for Santa Fe or to wave from the back platform of deluxe private cars.

Outlaws who signed no guest books but did visit or ply their trade in Lamy included infamous Black Jack Ketchum, the Ike Stockton gang (said to have numbered 110 men at the top of their record), Tom Ashton and Sawdust Charley, among the many. Train robberies were a constant threat, and Lamy had its share, though it never suffered a really spectacular one.

The natural hazards of a frontier town were not missing, including two bad fires. In one (March 24, 1909) the railroad depot was completely destroyed, but a new one was soon completed. This one still stands.

In the meantime, the little town of Manzanares, not quite two miles up the canyon from Lamy, gave up the ghost. It could not compete with this aggressive little neighbor on the railroad. The remains of Archbishop Lamy's chapel there are still discernable.

Having peaked in the 1930's, Lamy began to decline in the 40's when the new diesels no longer required roundhouses and extra locomotives to push them over Glorieta Pass. The Pink Garter saloon, directly across from the railroad station, began to see fewer railroad workers and more tourists. It had kept a mid-victorian decor. El Ortiz, the popular Harvey House, finally closed in April, 1940, and was soon torn down.

39

Quietly, one by one, buildings were abandoned, their windows going blind, and tumbleweeds piling high in doorways. A few hardy residents (today about 75) continued to make Lamy their home, motoring to jobs in other places.

Robert O. Anderson of Roswell bought the entire town (37.5 acres) several years ago and commissioned nationally known artist John Meigs to renovate the old Pink Garter. The cherrywood bar, built in Germany and installed in Lamy in 1881, has been hand polished to a new brilliance, and all the furnishings are in keeping, with authentic paintings and statuary of the period brought in from Amarillo, San Francisco and other places to keep the atmosphere of its heyday. The name has been changed to Legal Tender, and a growing clientele makes its way over the paved 20 miles from Santa Fe to have a cocktail and dine at Lamy.

Passengers for Santa Fe no longer seem surprised when the conductor tells them to get off here, although when Los Alamos was a secret project, scientists heading for "the Hill" were thoroughly bewildered, for they had only 109 East Palace or Box 1663 as an address, and they didn't even get to camp in Santa Fe, but were sent on the then rough road to — of all things! — a boy's school far up in the mountains. It didn't stay that way, of course, but Lamy has changed little except to get a bit older, a bit more tired, and the railroad force isn't quite as busy as it once was.

RAILROAD TRACKS at Lamy junction today.

VIII.

Truchas

The paved highway from Cordova to Truchas follows the crest of ever higher hills, twisting and turning as it climbs. The first view of Truchas comes from a turn on a lower curve, and the village looks like nothing so much as a scene on a Christmas card, a view of the Holy Land in which tiny adobe houses and log barns are silhouetted in clean lines against the towering Truchas Peaks where snow glistens at least eight months of the year. Perhaps it is a Holy Land, for at the side of the road stands a much photographed rough wooden cross, who knows how old? – a *Calvario* of the Penitente or a *descanso*, a resting place for prayer and meditation for long ago pedestrian funeral processions. Certain it is that this cross sets the mood for the village, a mood of peace, tranquility, brooding silence and serene age.

Actually, the village isn't as old as all that. It was founded in 1754 as Nuestra Señora del Rosario de Truchas under a land grant, chiefly to members of two families, the Romeros of Santa Cruz and the Espinosas of Chimayo, say Adams and Chavez in *Mission of New Mexico*.

Paul Horgan, in his *Centuries of Santa Fe* gives the same date but a different set of founders. He tells of the Indian troubles in the northern part of the state, raids so frequent and disastrous as to cause the intermittent virtual abandonment of Santa Cruz, Chama, Abiquiu, Ojo Caliente, Embudo and Chimayo. One settlement that held firm was Trampas where the settlers felt secure enough to foster a new settlement – Rio de las Truchas. It was built by government specifications with houses united and joined forming a square town site closed in with only one entrance wide enough for a single cart to pass through.

The town site sits on a high plateau with percipitious slopes down to the *rio* far below in the canyon. Water for household use and irrigation was necessary, and the families (local legend says 12 families) went over a league above the village and dammed the stream to a height of more than 60 *varas*.

From this backed-up water supply, they dug an *acequia* (irrigation canal) with the most primitive of tools and brought water to the village and fields. That ditch is still extant, though now the town owns a 280-foot deep community well, with a mile of pipeline, all powered by an electric pump. Five or six families have their own wells in addition.

CAMPOSANTO — cemetery — in the shadow of towering Truchas peaks.

MORADA at the side of the highway, an unusual location for this quiet religious sect.

It wasn't easy to get the little town established. In 1762 it was necessary to move the people from both Trampas and Truchas over to the parish of Picuris. After all, Truchas was on the edge of Comanche country! They must have gone back to their homes in fairly short order, for in 1772 another archive records the request of the villagers for 12 muskets and powder to be used for protection against the Comanches. "Denied" is written in answer to the request.

Courageously they stayed put, the thick walls and carved doors holding until at last the threat disappeared. These walls and beautiful doors have no metal hinges but instead swing on heavy carved wooden extensions of the door at top and bottom, firmly socketed in indentations in the door frames. A church was built, of course, but this old building, though still standing, became too small to handle the parish, and a new one has been built.

As the villagers realized that the old church was too small, and that a new one must be built, they also knew that they were not a moneyed community. Very well. They would, as their forefathers had done, build it themselves. Making adobe is slow work, but there were many talented hands. One woman with skillful hands came regularly on her crutches, for her hands were willing. Lumber and window glass were purchased at a cost of less than $5,000, and the cost of the church was just that. All the planning, labor and building was done by the community, so that now they have a $50,000 church, but no mortgage. The building reflects the love and faith built into it and is so constructed that it can be used for a growing community should the present trend reverse itself.

43

Looking at it, the visitor is prone to feel that this is, indeed, a mustard seed church, for the faith is here. The old church is now used for special holy day celebrations.

There is a public grade school as well as a Presbyterian school, a project that teaches weaving, and the Presbyterians have sponsored a unique Truchas doll-making commercial enterprise.

The Highway into and through Truchas had triggered changes. Until this roadway went in, Truchas was isolated and almost self-sufficient. The lack of easy access kept visitors out, and this same inaccessibility kept outside troubles away. A post office established in 1894 had Santiago Martinez as postmaster, the

OLD CHURCH at Truchas, used now for special occasions only.

HIGH WOODPILE guarantees warmth when winter snow flies.

office itself being in his general store. He kept this office until 1922, with his son taking over for a tenure of 40 years. The son is now retired, but the postmastership stayed in one family for 68 years, which should set some sort of record!

A sort of status symbol in this lovely little village is the size of the woodpile in the fall. There are a number of silver-colored butane tanks scattered here and there like beads from a broken necklace. Sunflowers valiantly try to hide these tanks behind green skirts, but where the homeowner keeps a tidy yard, they gleam grotesquely. Ex-Postmaster Manuel Martinez says, "We used to have lots of goats. We ought to have them again. They clean up trash and weeds."

With a good highway, well maintained, many of the people now work in Española, Los Alamos and Santa Fe.

Population is falling off in Truchas, as in the case of most of the mountain villages. It is now about half what it was even ten years ago. The season is too short for many crops, and the small farmer simply can't earn a living. With increasing frequency, the young people move afar to get jobs and follow a career.

Today, many steeply pitched roofs overlay the once totally flat ones since these roofs slide the winter snows off and cut down the maintenance required for the older flat tops. The village, with a Penitente *morada* close by the road and another set back in the fields, is a deeply religious one, one where brotherly love is not talked about much but is practiced without fail. Here the roots of grace and old fashioned goodness go deep. *Ricos* will buy up the old places, when and if they are sold, and the village life will disappear all too soon. But while it lasts, Truchas is a beautiful place.

ORNATE window facings distinguish this old home.

IX.

Wagon Mound

All over the nation there is an awareness that in the larger towns the center or core area is deteriorating, and an effort is being made to bring back the old vitality. In New Mexico we have urban renewal plans in Albuquerque and Santa Fe, ambitious face-lifting and plastic surgery for cities.

Out in the rural areas there are the same inexorable forces working, but little notice is given to small towns. The once lusty mining towns are written up in a plethora of books as ghost towns, and they rustle their shrouds for camera bugs and tourists. There is a sort of half-life in the recounting of their often violent, always colorful, careers.

Not so for the little towns that once served the citizens and countryside quietly, with no great fanfare, no historic battles or private feuds that stained floors with blood. No shining hour was theirs — these little John Doe villages, born of need, suckled with

THE WAGON MOUND, a landmark on the Santa Fe Trail.

faith and hope. For many, their dreams were slowly relinquished and then there was no one left to give them a decent, Christian burial. No camposanto exists for them.

For some there are a few crumbling foundations. For many there is only a windblown mound here and there in a landscape where mounds abound. Sometimes the selfsame wind that covered their bones uncovers a bit of willowware plate, a sun stained whiskey bottle, sherds of another time.

A few of these villages still exist, breathing shallowly, clinging to life and its vanities like great-grandfathers with eroded faces and palsied hands. They will reminisce, sitting in the sun, but their memories are vague, rambling.

Such a village is Wagon Mound. When the Santa Fe Trail was opening up, the distinctive shape of the mountain that over-shadows the village was easily recognized — a landmark. It could be seen from afar and resembled the oxen-drawn covered wagons that moved so slowly across the undulating plains. Today tourists ask, "Why was this place named Wagon Mound?" In an age of sleek cars and lumbering boxcar-sized trucks, there is no memory of canvas covered prairie schooners, and even when told, tourists answer "I just don't see it." Many have not seen a wagon, much less a prairie schooner.

Overnight camping here at the foot of the Wagon Mound was natural and easy. Sometimes when stock was tired they might stay several days — the black gramma and buffalo grass was thick and heavy. A broken wheel could be repaired, a new wagon tongue put in. Gradually a few people began to move out into the rich prairie land, bringing in herds of cattle and flocks of sheep. A few ranch houses, then more and more; a trading post and thus a village grew.

When the iron horse pawed its way over Raton Pass to the north and inched its way westward, there was a ranching community here. The plow had broken the soil, and sunbonneted women came in to buy baking powder, flour, sugar, calico and buttons. The old steam engines had to be watered and refueled at frequent intervals, and the Santa Fe Railroad put up a yellow station house, looking like all the others except for the name lettered on each end. Here, it was Wagon Mound.

Stores multiplied along the facing roadbed — a grocery, a smithy, a hotel, school — and stock and wool men built pretentious two-story houses with dormer windows. They even had a newspaper, *El Combate*. The main street and highway were one. Passenger trains stopped with clanging bells and hissing steam. Wagon Mound was a busy, proud little village. Teams were tied up along the street where ruts were deep in wet weather.

ONE OF THE FEW old homes which hasn't yet given up.

SATURDAY NOON on main street.

Times, however, were changing. The automobile began to arrive and leave, and the state began to improve the highways. Wagon Mound fought hard to stay on the highway — and lost. Railroad tracks had to be crossed twice, once to get in, and again to get out, if the highway went through town, so the new highway ran straight, even as the railroad had done. Wagon Mound was more fortunate than a lot of the small towns, however, since the road was now only across the tracks. When Dog Canyon cutoff was put through, the little villages of Optimo, Shoemaker, Valmora, etc., were completely bypassed, although the story goes that one rancher offered $10,000 to have the highway go through Shoemaker in a time when that much money bought a great deal more than it does now.

Passenger trains began to stop only when flagged, and then that, too, was discontinued. The hundreds of little ranches and farms began to disappear until now only a few big ranches are left — the Diamond A, the Mora Ranch and a very few others. Tractors replaced horses.

Even the new highway didn't stay put. A few businesses had moved across the tracks — a motel was put in, and failed. A garage and filling station prospered moderately; a small hamburger stand blossomed and attracted tired motorists — those who traveled the road often learned to like and trust their friendly service, and a break for coffee at this point was a natural.

Then the highway — which never seems to permanently make up its collective mind — moved yet again, tearing away the hill and

50

putting in an overpass. The little roadside businesses went too. The motorists were now over their heads.

There is a good school with around 15 teachers in Wagon Mound even today. Orange colored buses pluck children from the sides of the road for miles around. The town buildings, for the most part, have the battered grey look of the very old. Warehouses still stand bearing the honored names of Vorenberg and McArthur. Stewart McArthur, of the old and honored McArthur family, still ships wool and ranch produce out, but the Vorenbergs have left. Allan O'Dell, the last of the O'Dells here, no longer rides herd or runs a tractor. There is no one living on the old home place, and Allan runs a hardware and feed store. His home, across the street from the store, was built as a grocery store in 1886.

Frye's Hotel burned. A tornado ripped through the village in 1930, and some of the damage has never been repaired — sides of buildings torn away and now boarded up, like eye patches over a sightless, empty socket.

Where the main street once bustled, now few people move. Traffic on the new highway is swift, and scarcely glances at the old town dozing in the sun. There are still two passenger trains a day — one eastbound, the other west. Semaphores are always open and in an age of speed they no longer even whistle for a dying village.

SADNESS hovers about houses that once were loved and cared for but now stand deserted and overgrown with weeds.

X.

Lo de Mora

Mora is both like and unlike the other little Spanish villages that adorn the mountains of northern New Mexico. Mora seems to have had more of everything, good and bad, than most. On the good side more tillable land, water, game, close-by timber for building and fuel. The villagers also had more trouble with Indians, Anglos and with each other than most.

Today, the little village of around 800 straggles along both sides of Highway 3 between Las Vegas and Taos, mixing old adobe houses that stare impassively with sightless eyes, broken backs and weather-eroded flanks with trim, neatly painted modern cottages, cement walks and flower beds. The compactness characteristic of early villages is missing — not that it had not had this too, but the old village was practically destroyed by American troops in 1847.

There were probably settlers in this lovely valley before 1835, but officially a grant was made in that year to Jose Tapia, Carmen Arce, and 74 other grantees. Carmen was the daughter of Tapia, and that a woman (even a daughter) was co-grantee isn't common. The 74 sub-grantees probably came because Tapia promised them land, and Tapia must have known that he could not survive without the others. The valley was rich in all that they sought but was also the natural gateway toward Taos for the Plains Indians — Comanche, Ute and Apache. They raided Taos more or less frequently, and were nothing loath to pick up a bit more booty coming and going. Even if only going to Taos Fair, the Indians found the Mora Valley livestock made good eating, while the horses and mules took the weight off their feet and the produce was excellent.

The Mora country shows up consistently in archives and historical accounts. De Vargas went through on this natural trail, as well as the Villasur Expedition in 1724. Much later, this was the route taken by the Taos section of the old Santa Fe Trail.

Tapia came from Spain, via Mexico. He was married and had two children, Carmen and a son, the latter being killed by a bear. Tapia himself was eventually killed by Indians in Mora. It was not at all uncommon for the grantees to be attacked in broad daylight, says Eugene Hanosh in his Master's thesis (*A History of Mora, 1835-1887*, Highlands University, 1967) which can be read in the New Mexico State Library.

Traditional adobe homes were built in compact squares, with only a very few high, slit windows barred with small poles on the outside, and a patio large enough to hold the livestock during a raid if there were time to gather them in.

In 1843 a contingent of Texans under Col. Charles A. Warfield invaded New Mexico and there was a pitched battle at Mora. The Texans eventually retreated but left behind them many dead and the resultant seed of distrust for Anglos in any guise, Texans in particular. There are still traces of distrust of Anglos lingering today in the region. Treatment of the Mora people by later Americans was not such that this Anglo bias was completely dispelled. These people have fought too hard and too long — including Indians and Texans — to be placated with soft words. Their memories are very personal and are as long as the shadows of

LONG AGO residence of a *rico* is only partly occupied today.

the mountains surrounding them.

Kearny and his men marched close by but did not swerve for tiny villages — his sights were on Santa Fe. That was in 1846. In early 1847 there was an uprising in Taos, the immediate (but not underlying) cause being the arrest of three Indians for theft. Governor Charles Bent was then visiting his family there. It was a bloody affair, with Bent being scalped and others killed. Troops were sent in to quell the revolt, but Mora was then a part of Taos country, and they joined in the affair.

The day following Gov. Bent's death, some traders, Lawrence J. Waldo, Romulus Culver, Lewis Cabanne, a Mr. Prewett and a Mr. Noyes among them, were massacred in Mora under the leadership of one man called Cortez. Troops sent out were at first repulsed. Then, bringing cannon into play, they leveled the little town of Mora. This, too, was the work of Anglos, even though

55

they had taken Santa Fe without a shot being fired. Mora men were *muy macho* and did not capitulate so easily. This was, however, the last unified fight against the tide from the east, and the villagers went to work and rebuilt homes.

By 1885 it was a respectable little town site. Ceran St. Vrain, trapper, scout, soldier, trader, merchant, moved from Taos down to Mora to make his home. It was he who sold the land to the county (for the sum of one dollar) upon which the first courthouse was built. That courthouse is rubble today (just across the street from the Hanosh store), but the old jail and storage quarters still stand — they were at the rear of the courthouse complex. The Hanosh store was once the St. Vrain hotel, and the Hanosh family prizes furniture, books and other memorablia of that period.

St. Vrain bought up a great deal of land and put a flour mill, which stands today, and has been acquired by the county and city as a museum and civic center. Restoration is being carefully supervised. In addition to the mill, which furnished a great deal of flour used by Fort Union, St. Vrain also put in sawmills and even a small distillery.

He was very active in community life, and, when he died, he was honored with the largest funeral ever held in Mora, before or since. Fort Union soldiers attened en masse. He is buried in a private cemetery atop a small knoll about half a mile beyond the

PILES OF ROCK, such as this one near Mora, were used to mark boundaries.

ST. VRAIN built this gristmill in Mora. It is slowly disintegrating today.

Mora public school. A new tombstone, donated by the St. Vrain Valley (Colorado) Historical Society replaces the old one, chipped, broken in half and eventually carried away, only to be traced and returned to Santa Fe in 1971.

The peak of affluence in Mora would seem to have been during the period that Fort Union existed. Farmers grew grain which was milled in one of the five mills that were built in the valley. St. Vrain's sawmills provided lumber for the fort as well as for citizens for miles around, and salaries for the men who worked at them. Their sheep and cattle, as well as hay, had a ready market close by. With the Indian wars over, they no longer had to contend with that danger.

Hostility among a number of local secret societies grew up, mostly political in nature, though religion also was involved in at least some of them.

In the 1860's a priest, Father E.M. Avel, seems to have incurred the disfavor of members in one of these societies. The altar wine was poisoned one Sunday, and though Father Avel detected something amiss, the wine had already been consecrated. He told the congregation there was something wrong, but since the consecration had taken place, he drank it anyway. After mass he retired to the rectory, where stomach cramps soon assailed him, and he was dead in a few hours. Who poisoned the wine is still unknown.

The inner disturbances became so rampant that finding a body hanging from a tree was not uncommon, particularly during election years. People in Mora always have taken — still do— their politics seriously. The tenaciousness that made survival possible in the past is not gone completely.

Folklore is still repeated. The ghost of a Loretto nun is said to tell her beads in the modern church, built on the site of the old *camposanto. La llorana,* the crying wraith so common in New Mexico folklore, appears in the lore of Mora. What with the big universities putting in parapsychology departments, perhaps the world is catching up with what Mora has always known.

Certain it is that the world is finding out that the village of Mora is a fascinating place and the setting a lovely one. How it got its name is still a sort of mystery, though one account tells us that a French trapper (perhaps St. Vrain himself) on going through the valley found the skeleton of a man in the Mora stream. They called the place *L'eau des Morts* (Water of the Dead), and certain it is, however, that *Lo de Mora* is the name on old deeds and tracts.

XI.

San Miguel del Vado

San Miguel del Vado looks old and sleepy. It is both, although once it was one of the busiest places in New Mexico. In 1794 a group of 51 settlers camped on the banks of the Pecos River, now midway between Santa Fe and Las Vegas, while they molded the adobe bricks to build homes and a church.

Following Spanish precedents, they built houses around a plaza, with homes sharing walls with their neighbors. Long *portales* shaded the interior, but the outside walls were unbroken by doors, and the windows were set high up against the roofline and were very narrow. Some of these high windows still exist. Building this way was necessary, for roving bands of Apache, Ute and Comanche still were a threat.

The settlers wanted only to grow their crops and pasture their

DANCE HALL shows recent efforts of restoration.

59

sheep and cattle. The spot they selected was at a natural ford over the Pecos River. Here the swift-flowing current widened out and lost its urgency. The bottom is sandy, but firm, and heavy wagons and carts could cross without danger.

The little community prospered. The church, dedicated to San Miguel, was in the old plaza, and an artificial elevation (enclosed by a wall) was put in before the building was erected. That must have taken a great deal of work, for all labor and tools were completely manual. They labored well, for the church still stands, a rosy pink like a peach blossom fallen to the adobe red earth.

When Becknell opened up the Santa Fe Trail, San Miguel soon became a customs collection point. We are happy today that Albuquerque has been declared an international customs center, but San Miguel beat it by over a century.

Manned by Mexican soldiers, a complete customs station for the Santa Fe Trail was established in 1830 in San Miguel since some of the wagons headed for Chihuahua by-passed Santa Fe completely. Others were repacked, for the duty was computed by wagon load, and as much as could possibly be put on one wagon was — much more than could have been managed on the long trip

ONCE the home of a *"rico"* — rich man — now deserted.

SANTA FE TRAIL ruts grow deeper each year from natural erosion. Wagons once forded the Pecos River here, but the *vado* — crossing — is no longer used.

across the plains. San Miguel was a center, the gateway to a new territory for the Americans.

The Texas-Santa Fe expedition, bent on adding this territory to the Republic of Texas, was met and defeated near San Miguel, and the Texans imprisoned in this frontier post for a time.

When Gen. Stephen Watts Kearny marched into San Miguel in 1846, he talked to the villagers here as he had talked to people in Las Vegas before marching on to Pecos and then Santa Fe. San Miguel remained important as long as the covered wagons moved and was the county seat.

The coming of the railroad into Las Vegas marked the beginning of the end of the importance of San Miguel del Vado. Fewer and fewer wagons briefly disturbed the waters at the crossing, and the peak population of 1,000 gradually decreased.

Now most of the old adobe houses are reverting to the soil from which they sprang. The ancient dance hall had had some repair work done on it, but even that seems to have come to a standstill. A curio store, "The Cover (sic) Wagon" has a couple of gas pumps, and the old trail road, while plain to see, had been badly eroded by rain water and snow melt seeking to join the waters of the Pecos.

There is nothing left of the old courthouse but a rough mound of rubble and disintegrated adobe bricks. One house, west of the plaza, must have been the home of a "rico" — a wealthy man.

CHURCH MUST be built on higher ground, even if soil has to be carried in as it was at San Miguel.

OLD WALLS, showing vigas and soil above to shed rain and snow water.

Abandoned, the L-shaped structure still has the marks of elegance, although the doors swing in the wind, window frames have been pried out, and storms (or vandals) have torn away part of the rusted galvanized roof, a later addition, leaving skeletons of wooden rafters and *vigas* patterned against the sky. One room still has the box frame of a bed, heavy slats in place (remember they didn't have springs when such beds were used either!) Somehow this house seems more forlorn than any of the others.

With the Santa Fe Trail marking its 150th anniversary in 1971-72, San Miguel del Vado remains a quiet but dramatic link with that past. The church, a few houses still occupied, and the ghosts of walls tell of passed glory. The old *vado* (crossing) is used no more.

XII.

Valley of the Stolen Saint

It was Sunday, and the door to the little white church was not locked. There is a lock for it now, even though their chief treasure is gone. One night, when there was no moon and the village of San Ignacio slept, their hand carved *santo,* the San Ignacio to whom the church is dedicated, was hastily loaded into a pickup or car and carried out of the valley where he was so loved.

Somewhere — probably back east where they are just beginning to realize that a distinctive art form quietly grew up among a religious people who lived in tiny villages in New Mexico — the San Ignacio they loved is in a glass case, a museum piece to be bragged over. Perhaps the people who show the statue do not know that he was stolen from a small church in the mountains. The thieves must know now that he who drinks of a mirage finds his mouth filled with sand. Money gained by theft is always a mirage.

No more do the women of San Ignacio patiently sew their finest bits of material with the tiniest of stitches to make their *santo* a new garment, though they light a candle and pray that he may someday, somehow, return to them. They know that the best of the *santos* are being stolen, and that their's is gone. Their valley is the valley of the stolen saint.

San Ignacio is such a tiny village — little adobe houses carefully plastered anew so that weather does not eat at the vitals of the walls. Some of the people moved away, for the Mister found it necessary to get a money-paying job in Las Vegas, Santa Fe, Los Alamos, Albuquerque or even such far away places as Los Angeles or Detroit. The houses that no longer shelter a happy family die slowly, but they die, and gradually their only headstone is a section of wall or a native sandstone foundation.

The old mill wheel, just below the village, is there no longer. It was sold to Y.A. Paloheimo for his reconstruction of an old Spanish village at Los Golondrinas near Ciénega. They do not resent this, for now the water wheel will be carefully cared for, preserved, so that their children can go see it in actual operation. They will not take their home-grown corn and wheat to the mill, for modern times have made it more expensive than just buying *masa* and flour. Women and girls still take their baskets and spend an afternoon on the slopes gathering the plentiful oregano and

65

other wild herbs that make their kitchens smell better than The Ritz or expensive dining rooms in big cities.

Fields here have not sprouted the new crop of concrete and steel. At harvest time ears of corn have the shucks pulled back and are tied to the clothesline and to long loops of rope across the ends of houses for savory *chicos* during the winter months. Tops of onions are braided into strings so that the onion can dry evenly, and those not needed for the family be sold to supermarkets in Las Vegas.

Their San Ignacio is gone, but the village rests in the long shadow of Hermit's Peak, and these people have not forgotton El Ermitaño.

"I wish I could have seen him just once," a tiny little mother says. "My grandfather saw him. He was very wise! Once when my grandfather went to the mountain, he tied his horse and a burro at the bottom, for the path was too steep for them. He climbed up and met The Hermit who looked at him and told him he had

HERMIT'S PEAK from the road above San Ignacio

66

BIG WATERWHEEL, now at Rancho Golondrinas, once stood here.

better go back because the donkey had pulled the rope too tight around the horse's neck. He returned at once, but the horse was choked to death. How the hermit knew this we do not know but he did."

Leo L. Archuleta, who knew all these valleys well, told of the time when a small boy fell off the footbridge and was drowned in the stream that sometimes dawdles and sometimes rushes with violence and destruction. The village men searched for the tiny body for three days, but could not find it. Then they went to El Ermitano and though he had not been in that part of the valley, he took a stick and drew the course of the stream in the sand. "Here, on this curve, where the tree roots hold fast, the boy will be found," he told them. They searched, and the pitiful little body was found wedged tightly around the twisted roots.

Louis H. Warner, in his book *Archbishop Lamy* (The Santa Fe New Mexican Printing Corporation, 1936) tells the story of this strange man. Early in 1866 a religious man, evidently of Italian nobility appeared among the New Mexicans. To some he said that his name was Giovanni Marie Augustine. He was later known also as Juan Bautista Justrano. He had walked with a caravan from Council Groves to Las Vegas. Upon the mountain, now known as Hermit's Peak, he made his home. He was a religious, and people carried food to him in his cave on the peak. This cave, a mere hole, was too small for him either to stretch out or stand upright in. The tiny entrance, logged up, had protruding nails so that he must, of

67

necessity, be scratched by their sharp points when he crawled in. With his staff he scratched about on the side of the mountain until a stream of fresh, clear water gushed out. It still runs today.

His food seemed to consist of *atole* made with blue cornmeal. One Holy day there was quite a crowd on the mountain. and hunger rumbled under the belts of men, women and children. He fed them all from his small bowl of *atole*, but it was never emptied. This is the story told by one of the old men in San Ignacio, just as it was told to him by his grandfather.

The Hermit set up three crosses on the top of the hill, the one in the center towering over the other two. Perhaps the throngs of people who climbed the mountain to see him, talk with him, grew too large for the sandaled "holy man." He was essentially a recluse. So, one day, with only his staff and *atole* bowl, he set out for the southern part of the state. Someone told him of a cave high up in the Organ Mountains near Las Cruces. He was warned that Apaches still roamed these rugged mountains, but he went on anyway. He agreed to signal at the end of three days if all were well, and when no signal came, a group of concerned people set out to hunt for him. They are the ones who carried back the body, and according to Warner, he was buried in an unmarked grave in Mesilla. The peak he chose for his home while in San Miguel County carries his name, Hermit's Peak, and no grander marker ever marked one man's stay. for it cannot be demolished by time or vandals.

ROAD WINDS past the little white church dedicated to San Ignacio.

WOMEN VISIT at a ranch home.

The people of San Ignacio have not forgotten him. "Sometimes we climb the mountain just to remember," one says softly. "It is good to remember such men."

The people in this valley are gentle, kindly people. If some seem a bit suspicious at first, it is not that, but shyness. They listen to the sound of a meadowlark more intently than to the gabble of a stranger until they are sure they are not being mocked. Then they will walk along the road with you, show you the print of a deer hoof, pinch off a bit of growing plant and tell you a tea brewed from its dried leaves will settle a sick stomach. They know because it does it for them and it does for the sons and daughters who attend the university in Las Vegas.

Tito and Viola Martinez of Sapello travel up into this little valley to attend the church, and often during the summer months go on up to their cabins clustered around a series of small ponds, with a gurgling brook singing a lullaby between them. "The fishing is good here," they smile, "but just to sit and listen and breathe is better medicine than any clinic can bottle."

"We used to have some goats here, but the mountain lions got them all," Viola says. "Sometimes we see one, but not often. We do see deer and other game, and the ground squirrels are so tame they want to live with us! Birds build their nests under the eaves of the house, and aren't a bit afraid of us. Birds out here don't think the ceiling of a cage the sky."

There is electricity along the valley now, but the unpaved road

CORN DRIED on the clothes line in the fall becomes *chicos* for a winter meal.

is still narrow, winding and every turn shows a new aspect of beauty. Wild roses along one slope are always white, Mr. Salas tells us, but he can't tell us why. "Maybe it's because they like our white clouds and want to fly with them," he smiles.

70

XIII.

Valiant Village

Unlike the old river road at Velarde, U.S. Highway 64 runs high along the mountain slope, avoiding the rich bottom land precious for the growing of fruit.

The detour is an asset for Velarde's farmers, but a drawback for the hastening traveler, for he buzzes through, never knowing what a lovely village he's missing. Along the highway are a few stores and numerous fruit stands, but the lives of the villagers are not lived along the pavement. They live among the fruit trees and vineyards.

Between the highway and the Rio Grande, orchard after orchard tells the story of the foremost industry here – apple, plum, pear, cherry, apricot, and until the big freeze in 1970, peach. Most of the peach trees were lost when the temperature dropped to 35 degrees below zero. Carlos Romero lost 110 peach trees alone. New young trees were planted and they are now beginning to bear fruit.

When the orchards are in bloom, the whole valley looks like a spring corsage on the breast of the earth mother. The scent is more precious than the most expensive of perfumes.

Down in these orchards, unseen from the highway, nestle the old homes, low adobe structures for the most part, far too many of them falling into ruin. Velarde is an old village, older than Española, sometimes called "The Spanish Lady," 14 miles to the southeast.

The Velarde family in New Mexico dates back to Juan Antonio Perez Velarde, who migrated to El Paso in 1725. Matias Velarde, undoubtedly of the family, settled in this picturesque valley, just below where the gorge of the Rio Grande narrows and the climb to the plateau on the north begins.

The village was then known as La Jolla, or La Joya. Translated that means "gem." And it truly is.

The name change probably came in 1855 when the first post office was opened. As was fairly common for small towns in those days, the name of the first postmaster – David Velarde in this case – was adopted as the name for the village. Not everybody accepted it immediately, however. Carlos Romero, a long-time resident, recalls that in his youth people still called the place La Joya, even though mail was addressed to Velarde.

71

SHEEP keep weeds under control in orchards, provide wool for weaving and provide savory food for long winter months.

When Matias Velarde settled in La Joya, Santa Cruz, just downriver a few miles, was the second most important villa in the Royal Kingdom of New Mexico. Decreed *La Villa de Santa Cruz de la Cañada* it had been founded in 1695. Santa Cruz, close enough for infrequent shopping trips, also provided a market for produce and wool. The soil was fertile, the mountains protected the villagers from winter winds, and the Rio was there with water for irrigation. There was plenty of game and fish.

La Joya, just at the mouth of the gorge, was a resting place for travelers enroute to or from Taos. Perhaps Governor Charles Bent and his party tarried here at least a short time on their way to Taos in that fatal winter that led to his death during the Taos Rebellion.

Certain it is that Col. Sterling Price and his Missouri volunteers and dragoons moved north toward Taos in February in 1847. There was a skirmish with rebellious natives at La Canada (Santa Cruz), but the major brushes were at La Joya and Embudo.

When the rebellion had been put down and troops were no longer needed in such numbers in Taos, Col. E.V. Sumner, feeling that New Mexico towns provided a poor environment for troops, sent Major Gordon and his infantry company to La Joya for the

72

winter. But they had hardly finished getting settled when they were ordered back to Taos.

Velarde settled back into the quiet business of living, and men who were to become famous — Ceran St. Vrain, Kit Carson, et al — passed through Velarde on the old river road, en route to Santa Fe or returning to Taos from visits in the Ancient City.

Fruit trees were planted and thrived. Chili was a staple crop. Mrs. Rafaelita Luna (born in Velarde) recalls as the most exciting moments of her young years the times when wagons and trucks from far down the Rio came to buy or trade for chili and fruit. She owns a

MRS. MYRTLE WHITE ROMERO came to Velarde as a school teacher.

lovely native dye Navajo rug she acquired by trading chili with a Navajo.

"The weather is changing," Mrs. Luna says. "Now too often the chili crop is caught by frost before it can mature."

Mrs. Carlos Romero (Myrtle White), a resident of Velarde since 1929 when she came to teach at the tiny mission school, now writes of this area in a column in the Rio Grande Sun. A collection of her columns was issued as a book, "Housewife on the Rio Grande," in 1970.

"There hasn't been a bumper fruit crop since 1965," she says. "When our fruit fails, we're in trouble, for that's our cash crop."

This year, after a hard freeze before Easter, the village was in trouble again. "We're getting used to it now," says Mrs. Romero. "Last year there were a few apples left after the spring freeze. Then came the hail in August and made windfalls out of those." Even the apples have been ruined for 1972.

"It doesn't look like we're ever going to have fruit again. We're all discouraged," she says.

Velarde will undoubtedly survive this latest disaster, however, for although its community identity depends on fruit, not everybody works in the orchards. Many residents travel out of Velarde daily to jobs in Española, Santa Fe or Los Alamos. And some of the village's young folk commute to Santa Fe to the College of Santa Fe.

Velarde is a quiet, friendly little village, but outside influences are beginning to be felt. It is necessary to lock doors now, when until recently it was unheard of.

The orchards are well kept, with horses, cows and sheep grazing between rows of fruit trees. Men and women sometimes fish on holidays, " . . . but it does seem awful that I have to buy a license to throw a line in the river while sitting on our own land," Mrs. Romero says ruefully.

XIV.

Rociada

Say the name *Rociada* to yourself several times and listen to the music of the syllables. They sound like a sheep bell, far off across the *cienega* in early morning when timothy and foxtail grasses are wet with dew and the smell of piñon fires mixes with the more urgent odor of perking coffee.

Rociada means dew-sprinkled. This lovely valley, 22 miles northwest of Las Vegas, is well-named, for dew lingers until the mid-morning sun has shortened the shadows of the enclosing mountains.

Scattered here and there up the valley are little ranchitos, adobe houses that began with flat roofs and protruding *vigas*. Now many of these homes have steeply pitched roofs of galvanized tin to channel off summer rain and to help winter snow melt quickly and thus cut down maintenance of the earthen roofs.

There are three tiny villages in the valley, first settled by Jean Pendaries. Two are called Rociada, and the third is named Gascon after Pendaries' far-off native province in France. Lower Rociada was once called Santo Niño. The tiny church is still called Santo Niño, while the church in upper Rociada is dedicated to San Jose.

Oliver La Farge, Pulitzer Prize-winning author, did a book about the Baca family and the big Pendaries ranch here, since his wife, Consuelo, was the great-granddaughter of the founder. The book, called *Behind the Mountains*, is well worth reading. No one has yet done a book about the smaller ranchitos and the villagers, though they are just as fascinating.

The Canuto Ramirez ranch is the center of upper Rociada. Canuto now sleeps in the *camposanto* with two of his children, but his widow lives in a new, completely modern house just across the road from the old house. The old home also was the post office, for Mr. and Mrs. Ramirez were postmasters for 45 years. They also ran a small general store. The front room still has the shelving boxes for distributing the mail, which in a much earlier time came but once a week. Rociada got a post office in 1883.

Leroy Ramirez, now a prominent Santa Fe insurance man, grew up here, though he was born in' Mora. His mother was from Mora; she went home to be with her *Mamacita* when the natal day for a child grew near.

Rociada did not then — nor does it now — have a doctor. But Dr. Brown, of Valmora, was beloved in the valley. He bought land here (now the Davis Camp) and kept a paternal eye on the entire population. Every child was given a Christmas gift by Dr. Brown. He also gave special treats at the end of the school year for attendance and distributed very special ones for graduates. For parents, the doctor stocked blooded rams and bulls, so their flocks and herds could be upgraded.

The Ramirez ranch was well-equipped with barns, a blacksmith shop, sheds for farming equipment and all the other things needed for ranching when horsepower for labor and transportation was in horses. The buildings still exist in remarkably good shape.

The first electric lights were brought to the village by a wind-powered generating plant; the tower for it still stands gaunt against the skyline above the fruit trees. Millstones, once so

SANTO NIÑO CHURCH in Rociada.

76

SCHOOLHOUSE, where youngsters learned to spell and "figger," now shelters horses from stormy weather.

necessary, decorate the yard at the old place. And a now clapperless bell that used to summon the men from the fields is still firmly in place under a giant cottonwood tree — one that wasn't nearly so large when the bell was installed.

Mrs. Ramirez is a sturdy, but shy, quail of a woman, interested in all that goes on. She raised six children, only to have two daughters die of pneumonia within a day of each other. The two young girls were caught in a rain shower and developed bad colds that quickly turned into pneumonia. Antibiotics were then unknown, and the disease was often fatal.

Shortly after the death of the girls, a neighbor's wife died. Mrs. Ramirez quietly took a tiny boy home with her, for she couldn't bear to see a child so forlorn and bewildered. He did not leave the Ramirez home until he was grown, and his children are counted among her six grandchildren and 13 great-grandchildren, who visit the ranch frequently. The Ramirez children think of this boy as brother. Such a course in the valley was not rare, for the villagers lived the good neighbor tenets rather than talked about them.

While Leroy was a youngster there were only three families in the entire valley who were not Penitentes. There is a little gem of a *morada* in the valley, deserted now but still intact. This order has been badly misunderstood since writers centered on the Easter passion rites, completely overlooking the year-round place it had in the lonely frontier villages.

A regular priest came to the village church from Sapello once a month, weather permitting. But the Penitente brothers were there every day, helping a neighbor gather crops, chopping wood for a window or a disabled man of the family, caring for stock, sharing their own food and clothing when necessary, nursing the sick and doing whatever they could to help. Should there be a death, they quietly brought food, helped conduct the *velorio*, made the coffin, dug the grave, took care of ranch chores.

An Indian, Lame Deer, once commented a long time ago that Anglo Christians believed in suffering when it was somebody else and not themselves. But the old-time Penitente found solace for his soul in sharing, at least a little, in the suffering of the *Cristo* whom he so devoutly worshipped and tried to emulate.

The old schoolhouse, where Leo L. Archuleta was once a teacher, is partially a ruin. There horses find shelter when snow blankets the pastures. The schoolhouse was where neighborhood dances were held, with Papa, Mama and all the children gathered to celebrate betrothals, or just to get together.

Archuleta found, after several terms as teacher, that he would rather be a merchant. So he put in a store at Sapello. His daughter,

TINY MORADA, deserted, waits for the Brothers of Light to return.

MRS. CANUTO RAMIREZ and son, Leroy, at new ranch home.

Viola, and her husband, Tito Martinez (both born in Rociada), still run this store. Archuleta became court interpreter in Las Vegas.

Tito's parents have a store in the Santo Niño Rociada, in one room of their home. His family has run that store for more than 60 years. An overheated stove pipe burned it down once, but they promptly rebuilt it.

The elder Martinezes are godparents to 61 of the valley-born children, a function that is not undertaken lightly among people who care.

Both the store in Rociada and the one in Sapello are meeting places for friends. They stop in not only to purchase but to exchange news, leave messages for relatives, or to get warm when winter winds chill the bones of a rider or herder.

"Uncle Bustos," his sight and hearing not quite as keen as they once were, remembered one slight encounter with the Vicente Silva gang. As a young man, he was en route to Las Vegas one day with a load of hay. The gang came galloping up, demanding directions to a certain house. He drove his team with all possible speed through the dark night instead of making camp for fear that Silva's men would return, take his horses and leave him wounded or dead at the side of the rutted road.

There was no "youth" problem then – still isn't. Everyone knows everyone else. A grizzled grandfather will stop on the road to tell a high school boy how well he is doing with his own stock or that the price of beef this week in Las Vegas is pretty good if he wants to sell a young bull. He'll also stop with his big trailer when there's room for a couple more head if a neighbor wants to sell a heifer of two.

Some of the media often call the jet set on the eastern coast "the beautiful people." But they are so wrong. These village people are the beautiful people. Maybe they have never been on a plane, but they are the salt of the earth, the real strength of our land.

XV.

Watrous

Even historians lift an eyebrow when Fort Barclay, N.M., is mentioned. But there was such a fort at old La Juncta (sic) de los Rios, where the Mora and Sapello Rivers meet to gossip about what is happening in the mountains. We call the place Watrous now, a whole community that is an historic landmark.

Fort Barclay was never government supported, nor were there ever soldiers manning the two bastions. It was built at a cost of $28,000 in 1848 by Alexander Barclay and Joseph Doyle, two Colorado men who knew a good place when they saw it. The walls of the "fort" were 16 feet high, perhaps just a trifle higher than needed, but then this territory needed a bit more than the usual protection. The Apache, Ute, Kiowa, Arapahoe, Navajo and Comanche had been using this spot as a meeting place and campground for generations before the Spaniard, much less the Anglo, were heard of.

Perhaps Barclay and Doyle knew what had happened just five years before (1843) when a couple of men, one named Bonney, had attempted to settle here. Bonney was killed by Indians while searching for stray cattle in the Turkey Mountains. What happened to his nameless partner is not known, but that he didn't stick around is certain.

Barclay and Doyle were not completely happy here and advertised the fort, gristmill, cattle, horses, farming implements, etc. for sale in *The Santa Fe Weekly Gazette* of February 19, 1853. No one seems to have wanted it then, or had the money even with the

BLACKSMITH SHOP and stable originally well built so that the building remains in sound condition today.

liberal credit terms offered. Barclay died in 1855 and William Kroenig bought it from Doyle and lived there until 1868 when he moved over to the Phoenix Lake site. The fort was abandoned completely in 1879, and, staunch as they were, the last of the thick adobe walls were washed out in the big flood of 1904.

Barclay and Doyle were not without neighbors. Samuel B. Watrous, who had run away from his Uncle's home in Vermont when he was but 16, found a job on a wagon train from Westport to Santa Fe and stayed in New Mexico. He put in a store in old San Pedro while the gold mines were flourishing and married Thomascita Crespin. The confining duties of storekeeper had affected his health adversely, and, leaving Thomascita to run the store, he went off wandering in the mountains for several years.

METHODIST CHURCH retains dignity despite underbrush.

MASONIC LODGE claims to be the first in New Mexico, although Cerrillos residents claim their lodge was first.

The mines began to fail, so he picked up his family (wife, five daughters and two sons) in San Pedro and moved to La Juncta de los Rios.

The big 20 room house he built had space not only for living quarters, but a store, storerooms, grain and lumber rooms. The lumber for the house came by oxen drawn wagons from St. Louis, but the wrought iron work used was done right here. When Thomascita died (1856) he soon married Rosa Chappin. She died in childbirth and he married her sister, Josephine.

The house became a show place with a rosewood piano, gilded clocks and mirrors, buffalo and bear hide rugs, as well as Mexican furnishings brought in over the Chihuahua Trail from the south.

Watrous had not forgotten Vermont, however, for the long avenue of ancient willow trees that has charmed so many were planted by him from shoots brought from Vermont. These trees were not the only ones he planted, for cottonwoods were planted along the Mora River and as windbreaks, and his orchards were a community pride. Part of the orchard succumbed to the big flood of 1904. That flood must have been frightful − extending in damage from Shoemaker to well below Watrous, taking homes, trees, anything in its path right along for a swim.

Being a progressive man, Watrous donated $1,000 to help put in the telegraph line to Denver (1868), and it was he who gave the railroad right of way through his land and ten acres upon which to build the station house, etc. When the railroad had been built, it was they who changed the name of the village to Watrous over his objections. They had a La Juncta over in Colorado and did not want confusion to arise.

La Juncta (Watrous) was a stage stop for coaches on the old Santa Fe Trail and was one of the most progressive little villages in the entire Territory. When Fort Union went in, soldiers visited Watrous often (in addition to Loma Parda, Tiptonville and Las Vegas) and sometimes there was trouble between the civilians and the men in uniform.

Watrous spread his holdings over into Cherry Valley (later called Shoemaker) and in 1879 installed a woolen mill, powered by a water wheel. It was financially successful, but the sons and sons-in-law began quarreling over it. Watrous threatened to shut the whole thing down if they didn't stop their bickering. They didn't, so he made good on his threat. In 1884 "the water wheel on the Mora stopped forever."

The village prospered for many years, but changing patterns in population have had an impact here too. Kate Hand, "Miss Kate" as everyone calls her, has run the country store here alone since her brother's death in 1950. She came to Watrous in 1908 from Alabama where she was born in 1890.

"The rough days were over when I got here," she says. The Hand Merchantile store was built on the site of the first hotel to be built in Watrous. The hotel burned in 1917 or 1918 (many felt the fire was deliberately set, for the hotel was owned by a German-born citizen) and, when Leigh Hand came home from World War I, he went to work for Rankin Merchantile, then built his own store in 1922.

Miss Kate, about the size of a short half pint, has bright blue eyes and a very wide, generous smile. Her store is a Greyhound bus stop and they sent in a photographer a few weeks back to take pictures of the diminutive, white-haired country storekeeper and her place of business to be used in company advertising.

Next door to Miss Kate, an old, weathered sign says "McLaughlin Merchantile." A much smaller, free-swinging sign says "Antiques." Evelyn Kiker ran this establishment, crowded with everything from gasoline irons and Jim Beam bottles to old sheet music and myriads of dolls. Mrs. Kiker collected dolls and did a side business as a doll hospital. She was a seamstress and specialized in bridal finery. Priceless old pictures of Watrous were kept in a cardboard carton.

"Have you seen the old Methodist Church?" Mrs. Kiker asked. "It was the first one in New Mexico, built in 1885. When Bernalillo built a church we let them have the bell. Our church hasn't been used since 1930. The Catholic Church was built in 1900 and is still going strong."

She pointed across the railroad track. "See that scar in the mountain side? That used to be a lime pit. You couldn't see it from here when it was working because all the way up to the station house was piled high with stacks of cross ties and lumber. We had a sawmill too."

The schoolhouse, grades one through eight, was built in 1908 and closed in 1958. That same year (1908) the big livery stable that stands so gaunt today was built. It went out of business in 1916. The blacksmith shop lasted longer. A Mr. Thorpe opened it in 1880, and it wasn't closed until 1926.

An old Masonic Lodge building (without a cornerstone!) is a dignified patriarch. Both Watrous and Cerrillos claim to have the oldest Masonic Temple.

The new four-lane highway by-passes one of the quaintest villages left, and it's a shame that tourists racing by don't know what a charming bit of the past they are missing. The railroad (unlike highways) still uses the original roadbed, but the station house was torn down ten years ago. Faded letters on one old building say "Valley Hotel" with sleazy white curtains hanging limp and dusty from long since abandoned upstairs windows. The hotel bar became a saloon and was popular for quite some time before it, too, resigned itself to creeping decay.

OLD, OLD HOUSE still in use today.

A plaque in what was once a campground, later a city park, tells the visitor that the entire community is an historic landmark, so designated in 1964.

With Indian raids, a stagecoach stop, an important railroad shipping center (in the past) a once lively little village now slumbers with five cemeteries holding most of the real old-timers.

XVI.

Galisteo

The words "Valley of the Galisteo" have the lovely, lilting sound of old-fashioned poetry. The village of Galisteo, with its flat-topped adobe houses, low rambling rock walls and ancient , gnarled cottonwoods, fits into this valley as naturally as sandstone ledges. It is an *abuelo* village, a grandfather with all the dignity, grace and wisdom that comes with good breeding and long memories.

At this site the Tanos built nine pueblos, two on the north side of the meandering Rio Galisteo, seven on the south side. Five of these pueblos were occupied when Coronado's golden helmet threw back the arrows of the sun as he rode through in 1541 enroute to Pecos and the Buffalo Plains.

Gramma grasses of many moons covered his tracks before another Spaniard came in 1583. Espejo, ostensibly searching for the three padres but in reality searching for the metal of the sun that he hoped would buy pardons for himself and his brother on a murder charge, paused briefly. The treasure here could not be shipped back to Spain. He was one of the few that did not try to name the town.

Castano de Sosa, visiting here in 1591, named it San Lucas. Oñate, a scant seven years later, called it Santa Ana. While he was busy establishing San Gabriel, Fray Juan de Rosas, a Franciscan, came to bring the Cross to the Tanos in the valley. By 1617 the church of Santa Cruz de Galisteo was one of the ten churches established in what was to become known as New Mexico.

When Popé led the Indians in the Pueblo Rebellion of 1680, there was not time for Fray Velasco to reach Galisteo on foot from Pecos with a warning. He was struck down in a field near Galisteo, and Fray Domingo de Vera, Galisteo's priest, was clubbed to death in his own church. During the siege of the Palace of the Governors, the Spaniards there were sickened to see an Indian wearing the scarlet altar cloth as a belt. It told them that Galisteo had fallen.

It was 12 years before De Vargas reconquered the province and the Camino Real felt the tread of Hispanic feet surging north from El Paso del Norte. Among the settlers returning was an Hidalgo family named Ortiz. Because of their loyalty to the

WELL HOLE in the Ortiz y Davis patio, no longer in use, hosts a sturdy young cottonwood.

crown during the rebellion and their high social station, they had been rewarded with a large land grant in the Galisteo basin.

The mountains that loomed to the south became the Ortiz Mountains. and by 1703 the family had laid out the town site of Galisteo. Houses were thick adobe with walls that enclosed a patio large enough so that domestic animals could be driven in and protected during Indian raids. The walls were pierced only by loopholes and the big, heavy barred gate that was the entrance way.

A new church, *Nuestra Señora de los Remedios* (Our Lady of the Remedies) was built, and the Ortiz family was the patrón.

A trading post was built, and the history of this building reflects the tide of history in the town. In 1708 it became a dance hall-casino, the floors sometimes stained with blood. In 1712 the village was raided by Comanches and the women and children of the village were sheltered in the trading post while the men fought in the rock courtyard. In 1821 it became a Mexican Post, with the dragoons defending the east flank of the *Camino Real*. Then, 1846 saw the coming of the American Cavalry, and it became an outpost for them. Rebel troops invaded it in 1861 and in 1912 a rally was held here to talk of the new statehood.

The Ortiz name still reigns in Galisteo. The family home is but a short distance from the trading post, which is also a museum. The store and museum combination, run for so many years by

Frank Ortiz y Davis, has been taken over by his son, Jose Ortiz y Pino. In the museum there are family treasures and those of the surrounding countryside — Indian bowls from the Galisteo Pueblos, ancient *metates* and *manos* that the Indians left behind when they roved, the pipe collection of Frank Ortiz y Davis, many of which had come to him from notables.

A high point is the Padre's room where visiting Archbishops Lamy and Salpointe warmed their hands and slept in the big bed which has been carefully restored. Religious statues on the mantle above the fireplace date back to 1620. A macabre note is a child's coffin, with a glass viewing plate, that stands near the old cupboard filled with priestly vestments.

The courtyard in back of the trading post is still surrounded by the old walls, with a restoration and clean up bringing the whole complex into top shape historically and aesthetically. Soldier's quarters, blacksmith shop, an oratorio, an Indian prisoner "hole in the ground" that showed little compassion for its occupants.

The gringo invasion in 1846 under Stephen Watts Kearny's Army of the West left no visible marks on the town, nor did the Texas Expedition 16 years later.

Some of the old houses are deserted, walls crumbling and windows blind, but more and more of them are being bought by people who love the old village, and restored and made into lovely homes once again. Ballad singer-actor Burl Ives completely redid one of the old homes and once again made it the showplace that

FARM WAGON on the inside of the Ortiz y Davis patio in Galisteo.

it was in days gone by. The music of guitars is still heard softly strumming from the portals of old adobe houses, though candle-light is now for beauty rather than utility.

HOMEWARD BOUND, cow and calves are a familiar site along dirt roads in the village.

XVII.

The Hidden Valley

Arroyo Hondo

The green velvet ribbon of the Arroyo Hondo is cut by another ribbon of black asphalt that descends into the valley like a plumb line and climbs out over the hills behind it the same way, hurrying on to Questa or Tres Piedras. Engineers have tunnel vision and wear blinders to the whimsical little meandering roads, the beaver dams (now gone to beaver heaven), mounds of rock and dirt that nature has pushed up. They cut through the mounds, fill in the dips and make travel fast but uninteresting. Most of the speeding motorists watch the striped center line of the highway and don't see the lovely countryside at all. It's as though they were in a 3-D movie without the odd little pasteboard framed "glasses" that bring the jumble into focus.

Streets in Arroyo Hondo (Deep Ditch) wander willy-nilly and run up and down the valley, not across. Every little turn provides another living painting for the finest of all galleries. Small fields, log corrals, grazing sheep, cattle, horses cluster around adobe houses with Taos blue doors and feathered-with-age protruding *vigas*. Some houses have pitched metal roofs so common where snow piles high or rain falls in torrents — or not at all! Dirt roofs crack and leak at exactly the wrong time.

The village, with not one plaza but three, is not old as mountain villages go. Simeon Turley in 1830 saw the possibilities of the clear, cold little Arroyo Hondo stream and went there to make his home. There were a few settlers there then, but not many. He put in a water wheel and a mill to grind grain, and soon had spinning wheels and looms operated by the Mexicans who, with some protection from the Plains Indians, more and more came to settle above and below his rancho. He put in a distillery which was soon famous all over the frontier. Pink peach blossoms dropped their petals on the woolly backs of sheep, cattle wandered up on the hill pastures, and then the Americans came to New Mexico.

Kearny took Santa Fe without a shot being fired, but that did not mean everyone was happy at having the white-eyes take over the land. Carlos Bent was governor in 1847, and decided to make a trip home to Taos for the Christmas holidays. He had been warned but went anyway. There he was scalped while still alive, and the rebellion spread rapidly to Arroyo Hondo, only ten miles away.

Turley, too, had been warned, but he knew and liked his neighbors and felt that they liked him. One of his employees, Otterbees, who had gone to Santa Fe with a load of liquor, soon rode up to the gates at Turley's with the news of what had happened in Taos, and being a prudent man, he promptly galloped away.

Turley still felt safe, but agreed, at the instigation of his eight Anglo companions, then and there to close the gates and get ready to defend themselves. A few hours later a crowd of 500 Mexicans and Indians arrived and called out to Turley, telling him that if he would surrender his property and the eight men with him they would allow him to go free. Turley indignantly refused, and the battle began.

When dark came, the insurrectionists had the stables, but Turley and his men held the mill. The fight began again in the morning, with reinforcements coming from La Cañada, Fernando de Taos and other places. Turley and his men made every shot

OVERVIEW of Arroyo Hondo.

CANYON WALL shelters this old home.

MORADA, lower plaza.

count, but eventually two of his men were wounded. Then, since the walls of the mill were strong, the Indians and Mexicans began to try to burn them out. Several times minor fires were extinguished, but there was one they couldn't control. It was then every man for himself, and under cover of the billowing smoke Turley managed to escape to the mountains.

Here he met a Mexican man who was a friend of many years standing. Turley offered him his expensive watch for his horse, but the man refused, telling Turley to go to a certain abandoned rancho and hide. When dark came he would bring a horse and food to him. Turley did as he was told.

The Mexican friend rode immediately to the still burning mill where the crowds were looting the house and stables of everything they could carry and told them where Turley was hiding. They went to the rancho, found Turley, and weighted him down with bullets and arrows.

When the trouble was over, the natives settled down to farm chores and their normally peaceful way of life. They built five religious structures, though the population was never more than several hundred. Spanish families moved into the area, and two of these structures were built as family chapels, those of the Martinez and Medina families. Our Lady of Sorrows was in the upper plaza, with a *morada* of the Penitentes nearby. A *morada* also was built in the lower plaza.

The work of the *santero* — the saint maker — reached high standards here, with at least three doing outstanding work. With better roads making travel easier and faster, the need for private chapels and the *moradas* gradually decreased, and the Taylor Museum of Colorado Springs stepped in and bought up the major part of this unique art work. We hate to have had it leave New Mexico but are glad that it was saved and is well and proudly cared for in our sister state — not too far for us to go see.

Some say there are still Penitentes in Arroyo Hondo, some say not. They are a quiet, unpretentious people, and since their religion is not a "show", there is little or no talk about it. The *morada* on the lower plaza looks deserted, and we did not find the upper *morada*. We did find fishermen casting their lines into the water that cuts the lower end of the valley so deep before it empties into the murky Rio Grande.

Old homes spoke silently of early days, and we wished that Cleofas Jaramillo, who grew up here, was with us to tell us of the fabulous old families she wrote about in her book *Shadows of the Past (Sombras del Pasados)*.

Only once has the even tenor of the quiet days in Arroyo Hondo been disturbed since the burning of Turley's mill. A very small bit of gold discovered nearby brought in a horde of gold seekers. The little bit stayed just that — no more was found — and the gold-hungry men straggled away.

Irrigation ditches carry water from the Arroyo to the fields, and the people need no lessons in ecology. They care for the earth knowingly and the earth repays them. Many travel out for jobs in Taos and even further away, but the love of the green velvet valley is deep in them and there are no "For Sale" signs. Instead, new houses are being built of adobe, and the children play and wave a friendly salute to the hurrying world as cars speed by.

If a storm threatens during harvest, it is not strange to see a young girl, a virgin, running toward it, hands filled with salt. When she reaches the crest of a hill her arms spread wide in the sign of the cross, the salt sifting out in a like pattern as she gestures. Dark clouds roll, thunder rumbles, but the rain does not fall, nor does hail beat down upon the crops. Down in the fields men hurry to get loads of grain and hay into barns, while wind whips the skirt and glossy black hair of the maiden. Young lads crawl down from their tree houses and hurry home, where *Mamacita* has a good hot meal ready, and all heads bow as Papa says grace — they are thankful each day for their hidden valley and the quiet life there.

95

TORREON, or watchtower, on the Carson House at Rayado.

XVIII.

Rayado

Why is this village, about 11 miles from today's Cimarron (though it is older than Cimarron), named Rayado? Rayado, in Spanish, means "streaked". Was it because someone marked the site with lines drawn in the dirt where houses were to be built? That was a common practice. Or was it because of the nature of the streaked rock formations in the valley? Or, it just might have been because, when Maxwell, or Kit Carson or some of their men first saw the place, a band of Plains Indians with streaked faces (tattoo, scar or paint) were camped there, and they referred thereafter to the site as "where we saw the Rayados"? The valley, by any name, is lovely.

Wandering around Rayado today forces one to wonder what makes a village an enduring one, while others seem to decay away, rapidly or slowly. As a frontier village, Rayado had more help than most, yet as a village it is no more. Science says that rats that are underfed live longer, but life in any of the frontier villages was no lap of luxury, and agricultural villages all had to depend pretty much on what they could do for themselves for subsistence.

Truchas and Trampas petitioned for firearms, and the petition was denied, yet Rayado had soldiers garrisoned there at least twice.

Today Rayado doesn't look or feel like a village, for it isn't. Yet it does have a village background. The Kit Carson house has been restored by Philmont Boy Scouts of America and serves as a museum. One section out of the four that made up the sides of the Maxwell house enclosure is still in use — three sides are gone. The homes of the little people, people who tilled the fields, guarded the herds of cattle, horses and mules, are no more. Wide expanses of lawn are today mowed by a man seated on a power mower. Only the small church (with the crossbar on the cross missing) looks and feels like village. Even the *camposanto* is a mile away from the church. Rayado has always been different. Today it looks like a subdivision on the outskirts of a metropolitan area, carefully manicured to look like it isn't. Small town stores of an early day had false fronts piled high to make them look larger than they were. Today's Rayado is a false front of a village that is no more.

CARSON HOUSE view showing type of window often found in homes in isolated villages.

In 1845 Kit Carson and Dick Owens went to the Rayado district to put up a house, barns, corrals — the things necessary to begin farming in the lush valley. By midsummer they had accomplished enough that Mrs. Carson was baking bread in an *horno* built for that purpose, and her washing draped the scrub piñon and oak brush to bleach and dry. But it wasn't to last. In August word came that Fremont was ready for his third expedition, and Kit had promised to act as scout and guide. Kit and Owens sold their cattle, horses and sheep at a loss. Josefa (Mrs. Carson) went back to the Taos home, and Owens went with Kit to Bent's Fort to join the expedition.

Four years later Lucien B. Maxwell talked to Kit about settling down on the Rayado. Kit was "tired of the roving life" and felt himself growing too old to be gallivanting around. It was time for him to put down roots, stay put.

In February of 1848 Maxwell, with a small band of men, pack-trailed into the Rayado. Why this step was taken in February, when cold weather presented an additional hazard, is not known. They were held up in a snowstorm which cost them a mule before they even got there, but by early spring they did have temporary housing built with enough lumber to have three or four rooms. Maxwell then took off for Kansas to buy supplies for the new venture.

Returning over Raton Pass, the pack train was attacked by a band of Jicarilla Apaches who not only succeeded in driving off 30 mules and 50 horses, but managed to snag some of the supplies. The loss was set at $7,200. and in that day and age that represented a whale of a lot more buying power than it does today. Maxwell and his party retreated to Bent's Fort and decided to cross the mountains at Manco Burro Pass. Traveling wasn't easy, and Manco Burro Pass was no more kind to them than Raton Pass had been. This time it was Ute Indians, and Maxwell got a bullet in his neck. He had to come in to Santa Fe to have it removed, a rather painful operation, and it was some time before he was able to think about taking an active part in the Rayado settlement. It also was too late in the year to try to go back to Kansas for supplies. Besides, money to buy them was short after the loss on this trip. He did manage to sell hay to the Army and some grain supplies to travelers on the trail to Taos, weathering through his spell of bad luck.

In the spring of 1849, Carson joined Maxwell on the Rayado. By summer, 40 or 50 men were busy at the site, lumbering, cutting hay, tending cattle, sheep and horses. Four farmers set about tilling the soil and putting in crops. The land (belonging to Maxwell's father-in-law, Beaubien) was not sold but worked on a share basis. Carson built a 17-room house about 100 yards south of the Maxwell house. High walls protected both the Maxwell and Carson houses, and the Carson house boasted a *torreon* or watch tower as well.

It was this house that the Boy Scouts restored in 1949. Only three rooms remained when reconstruction was begun, but they

MAXWELL HOUSE, partially reconstructed, as it is today.

had the help of Narcisso Abreau, who had lived in the Maxwell house and spent much time in the Carson house as he grew up. Abreau made rough sketches from memory, and when workmen began to clear away the debris, they found abundant substantiation of his memory. The complete restoration was accomplished and the museum, as it now is utilized, is basically the same as it was when the Carsons lived in the house.

Carson also planned to establish a trading post and to sell mules to travelers on the trail. Sporadic Indian raids in the whole area continued and it was decided to station ten mounted troops under William C. "Leigh" Holbrook at Rayado for the protection of the entire frontier. By 1850 this contingent of troops was increased to 43 men with 45 horses. Tents were used for a short time until arrangements were made to quarter the men in the Maxwell house. Rent on the quarters was set at $2,400 per year in the beginning and soon went to $3,400. In addition, Maxwell sold the Army hay and grain. It made this Army outpost a bit on the expensive side, and when Fort Union was opened the troops were transferred down there.

Indian troubles continued and wild rides to Fort Union for help were often necessary. In 1854 the Army once again stationed 61 men under Lt. J.W. Davidson at Rayado for a bit over two months, and then they once again went back to the Fort.

Rayado continued to grow until in 1857 Maxwell decided to move to what is now Cimarron. His ranch there prospered, and the mill he built when the government located the Ute and Apache Indian Agency there still stands and is used as a museum.

Rayado began to slip and diminish until today there are less than a dozen people who call Rayado home. The Boy Scouts use the site for an individual training center, the Utes are on a reservation in Colorado, the Apaches on another centered in Dulce, and the shouts heard during the season are those of sports, not the fear of raids that once made village life there a tense one.

OLD RANCH HOME with proud fruit trees.

XIX.

Ojo Caliente

Always in Hot Water

Three large pueblo ruins within a mile and a half of each other on the mesa above Ojo Caliente ("hot eye") attest that the Tewa Indians knew this spot long before the arrival of the Spaniards. The Tewas called these pueblos Homayo, Houiri and Pose-Uingge. The hot springs at the base of the mesa, they believed, were the opening between two worlds — this one and the one down below.

A story is told of Pose Yemo, born here to a virgin who conceived when a piñon fell on her lap. After years of poverty, Pose-Yemo became chief of the tribe and the vicissitudes yielded to a time of plenty. But after he left, the "walking water" (rain) did not come. Enemies did, and ruin followed, causing the pueblos to be abandoned.

Pose-Yemo, it is said, still returns one day each year, however, to visit his grandmother who lives in the pool where the "green springs" bubble up. The stones in the spring turn green from the

101

minerals in the water; the odor caused the springs to be called "stinking green water."

The Indians believed in the curative powers of these waters, and people from all over the country come in today for the same reason — to be helped by the invigorating liquid that still gushes forth, enriched by arsenic, iron, sodium, lithia and soda.

The exact date when settlement began at Ojo is not clear. There was trouble over land ownership as early as 1735, when a lawsuit was filed. Unfortunately, the location was on the frontier of the land roamed over by Comanches, Utes and Apaches, and living in the area was hazardous indeed.

In 1748 Ojo Caliente was a co-signer, along with Abiquiu and Quemado, in a petition to Governor Codallos y Roybal to evacuate; their petition was granted.

But by 1751 a new governor, Cachupin, was in office. He ordered the settlers to go back to their homes in Ojo. They were allowed only two months to comply, plant their crops and repair their houses. Some of them petitioned for more time, while others flatly refused to take their families back because of Indian danger. The government, however, rejected their fears. A fine of 25 pesos was levied for refusal to obey, and later this was increased to 200 pesos. Officials wanted settlers in the Ojo area to create a buffer to the more populous areas, such as Santa Cruz.

Permanent settlement was still avoided, though, for in 1768 Gov. Mendinueta declared much of the land unappropriated after he had made a personal visit. An official suggestion that the home sites be located on the mesa was negated because of the water problem. There wasn't any of that precious commodity up on top of the hill.

The community became fairly well established in 1790 when Jose Manuel Velarde petitioned for permission to move to Ojo Caliente with 18 families. They did not have enough land to support themselves in Bernalillo. Official approval was given on condition that the colony be heavily fortified because of Indian raids.

Small fragments of fortifications can still be found in Ojo by the alert visitor, or more easily if a resident points them out. The town, built across the river from the springs, was vulnerable to Indian attack from the precipitate cliffs above.

Zebulon Pike, brought through Ojo after his capture by the Mexicans, wrote a vivid description of the little village in 1807. The old church he described still stands, defying the ravages of time. A new church — a nice one — has been built, but it doesn't have the ancient feel, for it isn't. The hand-carved corbels, and knowledge of frightened women and children kneeling and praying

TRADITIONAL MOUNTAIN village home sporting a huge woodpile, as much a status symbol in remote New Mexico areas as a new stationwagon in a suburban driveway.

in the sanctuary of the old walls during raids, give the venerable adobe and stone of the deserted old church a strength that no new edifice can challenge. In 1957 a concerted attempt was made to raise funds to restore this old church, but the effort was unsuccessful.

Ernest Ingersoll visited Ojo in 1883 and wrote about the village in his book *The Crest of the Continent*. He was too eastern to appreciate the *santos* and *bultos* in the church — found them ugly and depressing. Ingersoll would surely not have understood the thieves who are making the raids on churches and *moradas* today.

Another man who wrote about Ojo Caliente was James W. Steele. He had spent some time in Army posts on the western frontier, and in 1873 published a book called *Frontier Army Sketches*. Steele wrote the sketches in fiction format but said they were not inventions or figments of the brain.

One of the most poignant of these stories, called "Brown's Revenge" tells of an Englishman named Denham who ran the Springs Hotel. Denham was a quiet man, one who never wore a gun. He was always a good, though mysterious, neighbor. He never talked of his past or where he had come from.

One evening, the story goes, a drifter, a range bum, showed up at the hotel. In yarn swapping he related that he once had worked in California gold fields, managing to acquire $10,000 in dust. Then he decided to go back home to his old lady and children, and

POST OFFICE, the meeting place of the village.

had exchanged the dust for thousand dollar treasury notes. But one night on the train, the drifter continued, the money had been stolen as he slept. He couldn't face his family in shabby clothing, with nothing to show for 12 years absence, and so he'd gone on the bum.

At this point Denham, looking ill, brought out a paper. It was his will, and he read it to the group around the fire. He'd been a poor minister, he recalled, and one night on the train he had seen this rough-looking character with the treasury notes. Thinking of his family and what this could do for them, Denham had stolen the money and hidden it in a bar of soap. A search had been made, but since the notes could not be found, the man, one William Brown, had not been believed.

The minister, however, had found himself unable to face his wife and children with his stolen gains, and quietly he'd dropped out of sight, refraining from communicating with his family or friends. In his will he was giving everything he had to Brown.

Denham tried to give Brown the money and deeds to the property, the storyteller says, but Brown refused, saying he had no wish for it any more, for there was no one to spend it on. Cursing the minister, he stalked out, and ". . . when the frosty sunlight streamed through dusty panes in the early morning, the face it shone upon was a dead man's waxen mask". Denham had become a suicide.

Many famous people have visited Ojo and its rejuvenating springs. Today a small, attractive hotel, cottages, bathhouse, treatment quarters, and a swimming pool are owned and operated by a small corporation, supervised by Philip and George Mauro. They came to Ojo in 1938 and built the first bridge across the river, which is generally shallow and gentle, but can be rambunctious when heavy rains swell it into a violent, muddy torrent. The author Ingersoll rented a donkey to get across, and there are stories that once there was a rowboat ferry.

Today the town sprawls along both sides of the highway, old and new houses scrambled together, and all friendly. The old Carlos Hernandez house (now owned by Coulter) is a charming motel called The Black Locust. Pete Lucero, great-grandson of a founder, runs a grocery store. Dan Joseph Jr. has a co-op crafts shop; Vern Byrne, originally of Santa Fe, has an attractive rock shop, and out in the valley there are still the Archuletas, Alires, Valdezes and Pachecos — their roots down deep into the soil.

The Mauros, steeped in the lore and love of the countryside, chortle as they tell the story of Billy the Kid swimming in the pool yet keeping his powder dry, his holsters on the bank within easy reach.

GRANDMOTHER HOUSE and well at Spanish village site.

XX.

El Rancho de las Golondrinas

While the silver cord for mountain villages is badly frayed, all is not yet lost. A Phoenix-like village, rising from the ashes of the past, is growing steadily and surely at El Rancho de Las Golondrinas, 14 miles south of Santa Fe at La Ciénega.

Las Golondrinas is a living museum of some 400 acres, with the old mountain villages giving of their heritages, insuring that they shall not be forgotten. The ranch itself was a *paraje*, a rest stop on the oldest road in these United States, the *Camino Real* running from Taos to Santa Fe to Sonora and Guadalajara.

Las Golondrinas (The Swallows) is the property of Y.A. Paloheimo and his wife Leonora, nee Curtin. Paloheimo came to the United States from his native Finland as a commissioner-general to the World Fair of 1939-1940. It was in New York that he met and fell in love with Leonora Curtin of Santa Fe, and she with him. Paloheimo soon became a man with two countries, for his love for his native country remains strong, yet he loves this one too, just as Mrs. Paloheimo has learned to love Finland.

The ranch at Ciénega was Curtin property. In looking over the buildings on the ranch, it became apparent that extensive repairs or new buildings were needed. Architect John Gaw Meem suggested a restoration, and when the Paloheimos became really interested in such a project, every step led them more enthusiastically. The ranch house was restored, even unto the *torreon* (watch tower) so necessary for protection in isolated locations long ago. About this time the Curtin home in Pasadena was named an historical site and the couple was really in the museum business!

The ranch house restoration, extensive though it was, was only a beginning. The Paloheimos began haunting the mountain villages for mementos of the past. "We were really too late for many, many things," Paloheimo says, "but there still were such things as buildings, heavy old equipment, things like that."

No doubt startled home owners were surprised when the tall, aristocratic looking gentleman and his petite wife approached them wanting to buy, not their beloved land, but an old mill, ancient hayricks, even old pigsties. Having been purchased, each part was carefully marked, the buildings disassembled only to be rebuilt on the acres at Los Golondrinas exactly as they had stood in their native village. Wisely, they were not set up in exhibition order, but carefully distributed where they naturally belonged on a working ranch.

And, working ranch it is, with fields of sorghum cane, vineyards, fruit trees, alfalfa, wheat and corn. The cane is cut, crushed the old way with a mule walking around in a circle while the ancient bucket hangs beneath the primitive crushing apparatus to catch the sap. Nearby is the long, shallow metal tank atop an elongated fireplace for cooking the sap, making molasses which can be further cooked into brown sugar. When a "Harvest Day" is

MULE stands ready to press sap from sorghum cane.

COOKING cane sap to make molasses.

held, the public is invited and young children love this spot best of all, for they are free to chew on cane stalks, the first time many of them have ever seen cane. On Harvest Day, or when a group of school children or visiting educational groups are there, everything is working and visitors can see, ask questions and begin (for those who live here) to know how their ancestors did their daily work. Of such knowledge, pride of ancestry is born.

Education groups can make arrangements for visiting any time of the year. The public in general can visit on special days which are announced well in advance. Crowds are heavy on these days.

In the old ranch house the furnishings are authentic where possible. When originals have not yet been obtained, duplicates are fashioned as authentically as possible. Outdoor ovens are heated, and native women bake bread, prepare chocolate and *biscochito* just as they did long ago. In another part of the house others work at the looms, weaving, carding wool, dyeing with native dyes.

A little way down from the main house wheat is being threshed by driving a herd of ranch owned goats over the scythed grain as it comes in from the fields. Grain is winnowed by tossing it into the air to rid it of chaff. In the big mill, powered by water, (the water wheel so well balanced it could be turned with a garden hose!) wheat is ground on huge millstones, and whole-wheat flour can be purchased. A smaller mill grinds corn, and visitors can watch the whole process. There are four mills on the ranch, no two exactly alike yet all authentic, including the original mill that was on the ranch to begin with.

There also is a wheelwright shop and a blacksmith shop — everything manned and working by people from the villages. Smoke rises from ancient fireplaces, with man-sized bellows for raising the heat of the fire, and wooden tubs of water for the quick dousing of homemade horseshoes or metal wheel rims.

Across the valley is another home with a *torreon* overlooking the vineyards and wine press. In a secluded nook is a small reconstructed village, with a grandmother home, completely furnished even to handmade quilts and coverlets on the beds, and pots of geranium and herbs on the deep window sills. Barns, outhouses, corrals are all in keeping. This was the way it once was in the mountain villages — the well yielding cold, clear drinking water, the hayricks piled high to feed ranch goats, mules, sheep and cattle. All is so well-maintained, clean and orderly that not even the most casual visitor would dream of throwing a cigarette butt or gum wrapper on the ground. We noted an empty bright yellow film box drop unnoticed from a photographer's gadget bag, and the boy just behind him promptly picked it up and put it in his pocket.

All the work going on at one time means many people working, which is the reason the museum must be seen by appointment or on an open house day. Work goes on in-between, but not everything at the same time.

Seminars and group educational meetings are held here, with the ranch being able to "sleep" 12 adults, plus 30 youngsters who

THRESHING WHEAT with goats at Ciénega Living Museum.

have sleeping bags.

Although it is a living museum, there is no feel of "museum" about this rancho. It feels as though one had stepped through a door in time, back 300 years, when life was much simpler (and more complex) in so many ways. This is living Spanish Colonial history, and this rancho is a member of "Living Historical Farms and Agricultural Museums Associations," national and international, sponsored by the Smithsonian.

Paloheimo, always interested in youth, is sincere and enthusiastic about the project. "Young people here don't understand what a rich culture they have," he says seriously. "We hope to show them, so that they will not only understand, but be proud."

He has not stopped dreaming, hoping eventually to have native arts and crafts operating, and the museum adds new features constantly. A low, rolling hill is now topped by an authentic morada reproduction that is beautifully done. The graves are not authentic, but markers are, as is the *descanso* (resting place) just below the crest of the hill. All who love the villages are grateful, including the villagers who gladly come at Paloheimo's call. They too, are developing a pride in demonstrating old skills.

WATER to run mill (background) is channeled through flumes made of hollowed logs.

111

WATERWHEEL at largest of the mills. *(Photo by Marsha Zucal)*

Index

114

Meigs, John, 40
Mendinueta, Governor, 102
Mesilla, 68
Methodist Church, 84
Mexican Post, 18, 21
Mexico, 21
Mina del Tierra, 6
Mitchell, 6
"Missions of New Mexico", 41
Mora, 75
Mora, Leo, 5
Mora, Mary Tappero, 3
Mora River, 81
Morley, W.R., 20, 23
Morley, Mrs. W.R., 23
Mora Ranch, 50

N

Nambe, 10
National Hotel, 20
Navajo, 7, 81
New Mexican, 10, 45
New Mexico's 200th, 34
New Mexico State Library, 54
Nick-o-Time Mine, 6
Night Riders, 27
Normal School, 25
Noyes, Mr., 55
Nuestra Señora del Rosario de
    Truchas, 41
Nuestra Señora de los Reme-
    dios, 88

O

O'Dell, Alan, 51
Ojo Caliente, 41, 101
Onate, 87
Ortiz Mountains, 88
Ortiz y Davis, 88
Organ Mountains, 68
Ortega Family, 32

Ortega, David, 32
Ortega, Nacacio, 33
Otterbees, 92
Our Lady of Sorrows, 94
Owings, Nathaniel B., 10
Owens, Dick, 98

P

Palace Hotel, 2, 3
Palace of the Governors, 2
Paloheimo, Y.A., 65, 107, 108
Parker, Michael, 28
Pecos River, 60
Pena Blanca, 5
Pendaries, Jean, 75
Penitentes, 9, 41, 46, 77, 78,
    94, 95
Phillips, Daniel A., 38
Phillips, Waite, 21
Philmont (Boy Scout Ranch),
    21
Phoenix Lake, 82
Picuris, 7, 9, 43
Pike, Zebulon, 102
Pink Garter, 39, 40
Popé, 87
Pose-Yemo, 101
Pose-Uingge, 101
Price, Col. Sterling, 72
Prince, Bradford, 3
Presbyterian School, 44
Prewett, 55
Procter, Charles, 28
Pueblo Rebellion, 87

Q

Quemado, 102
Questa, 91

R

Ramirez, Canuto, 75
Ramirez, Mrs. Canuto, 79

Photo by Bob Dimery

So completely and voraciously does she attack everything in life that interests her, virtually every hobby has become a profession for Alice Bullock. To describe her and the energies she generates is to search the Thesaurus for more and more exotic words, none of them ever very sufficient. As the end of it all, you simply have to say Alice Bullock is an energy force all her own.

She came to New Mexico at the age of eight in 1912, the year of New Mexico statehood, and since then the new state and the new resident have developed, changed, learned and produced together. Spending her early days in the coal camps of northeastern New Mexico, Alice became a teacher, moving from community to community to teach in one-room schoolhouses heated by pot-bellied stoves stoked by the older pupils.

When the Depression forced her out of the classroom, she and husband, Dale Bullock, bought the *Reporter,* a small weekly newspaper in Raton, and Alice was launched on a long, although interrupted, newspaper career.

The Bullock family, including two daughters, moved to Santa Fe. Alice opened a dress shop, began designing her own fashions and before long was selling dress patterns to major manufacturers. After retiring from this, she went into oil painting and was honored with several one-man shows before her health finally curtailed that career.

Alice became a free lance writer, then wrote a novel based on life in the coal camps. Later, she began writing newspaper features, developed an interest in photography so she could illustrate her own stories and finally wrote a book on legends of New Mexico. *Living Legends of the Santa Fe Country* is in its fifth printing.

Alice "ain't getting any younger," as she puts it, but you couldn't tell by watching. She is on the road often to this or that remote spot in New Mexico tracing down a legend, an interesting feature story, a colorful old character or some puzzling phenomena. On any day she might announce plans to go to Greece or Mexico or Arizona or somewhere else "just because I wanna."